Framily (friends considered ⌐ historical fiction trilogy by author, Lou ᴊᴀᴜ... ... of three childhood best friends commenced with the book,

"8" Center Field in New York, 1951-1957

- "Enjoyed it and gave it the highest compliment, I passed it on." *-Bill Lyon, now deceased venerable sportswriter of the Philadelphia Inquirer*

- "8" is a funny and heartwarming tale of growing up in New York City when a baseball debate took center stage through the eyes of three youngsters." *– T.A. Olsinski Death by RX, When Killers Collide, Attack of the Lambs*

- "8" masterfully fixes its lens on the lives of three young boys coming of age in a time before play dates, Facebook or cell phones were even imagined." *– Robert Ludwig, retired New York City school teacher.*

Dopey Bastid followed

- "Saulino is a talented story teller, and the way he mixes sports stories with those of the group of friends is smart and inventive." *–Kirkus*

- "Many of the interactions are genuinely amusing and evocative of New York in that time period, and the author's perspective on legendary sports figures is engaging." *–BlueInk*

- "Saulino can write good dialogue and create believable settings." *–Clarion*

Now, for the finale: *Framily (friends considered family)*
Kirkus applauds "This book is also immaculately researched, vividly recalling each play of each game like a great sports announcer....readers needn't be sports fans to enjoy the work; even those who are athletically challenged will be engaged by what is at its heart, a tale of love."

FRAMILY

FRAMILY

Friends Considered Family

Scala family
All the best
Enjoy! *Lou Saulino —*
May 2024

LOU SAULINO

Lou Creative

imagination not imitation

To my good friends whom I consider family. Thank you for being there for me.

FRAMILY

(friends considered family)

CONTENTS

INTRODUCTION

FRAMILY: Friends Considered Family is the third of a trilogy. It continues the sports discussions and escapades of three close friends since childhood, each now reconnected with their first loves.

The saga began with **"8" Center Field in New York, 1951– 1957,** as three thirteen-year-old amigos argued about the best center fielder in New York in their 1957 eighth-grade class. Was it Willie, Mickey, or the Duke? *Dopey Bastid* follows a reflection of the friends twenty years in the future as one buddy, with the assistance of his pals, writes a novel about dumb decisions in the world of sports. How was it possible that Ted Williams was deprived of the MVP Award during the year he hit over four hundred and in each year he won the Triple Crown?

FRAMILY commences at the conclusion of *Dopey Bastid*. The scene is a 1979 New Year's Eve celebration and concludes in the early summer of 1987. The sports stories herein are authentic, albeit with the addition of the perspective from an author who is writing about the events several decades afterward. Historical fiction is the genre.

The sports discussions continue in a format that author, T.A. Olsinski, had previously described as "the famous retelling reminds the reader what it is like to hear stories from the friendly guy sitting next to you at the bar."

FRAMILY has a diversity of historical event dialogues in various sports, inclusive of baseball, football, basketball, hockey, boxing, golf, and tennis. You will also share in nonsport history, such as the premature death of the comedic genius John Belushi, the movies of the era such as *Chariots of Fire and Stand by Me,* and the recollection of the music and poetic brilliance of Bob Dylan, Paul Simon and Billy Joel.

My intent is for you to either fondly recall sporting events or perhaps become more familiar with them. Moreover, the life events of the protagonists, Joey Kowalski, Bob Murphy, and Lou Marciano, along with their mates, will hopefully have you laughing out loud, shedding a tear, and most importantly reflecting on the true meaning of friendship.

ACKNOWLEDGEMENT

I would like to thank several people who were instrumental in reviewing and offering constructive comments regarding *FRAMILY*.

My brother, John, my cousin, Roger, Jim Luker (the misguided Boston sports team rooter, lol), and Joe Carriero (my buddy from Manhattan College) were all extremely helpful.

Once again, it comes down to family and friends.

CHAPTER I

COOPERSTOWN BOUND

1

Happy New Year! 1979 had arrived and the core six was quite up to the task of partying, save for one exceedingly pregnant Susan Kowalski. After the New Year kissing extravaganza and the offering of health and happiness to all, Susan proclaimed with a gleam in her pretty blues and displaying a broad smile, "I can go about another hour, you guys, and then it's time for my head to hit the pillow."

Janet and Grace, the two girlfriends, thought of as sisters by Susan, concurred, each offering a comment.

"Whatever you need to do, Mrs. Kowalski."

"Hey, that could be Grace Janet Kowalski in that belly of yours, easy does it."

Joey, the soon-to-be proud father, didn't push the fact that he wanted to party for several more hours. He understood his obligations as a prospective dad and knew he had to be content with one additional hour with his best friends, Bob and Lou, and their soon-to-be better halves, Janet and Grace. "OK, honeybunch. Damn, times have changed now that you have a little one in that belly. You used to be able to outlast me easily."

"Big deal, Kowalski. Mr. Three Drinks and Out has a freakin' revelation." Bob Murphy had drawn first blood.

Lou Marciano instantaneously reacted, "No shit, Sherlock, Susan could always drink you under the table. By the way you were talking about drinking, weren't you?"

The sexual reference evoked a giggle from Susan and a comment from Grace: "What did you say, Quickdraw?"

Dopey Bastid, the recently completed sports book of Joe Kowalski (Joey used the first name Joe professionally) was then discussed. Bob was insistent that Joey read the dedication. He and Lou had been privileged to share Joey's sincere tribute while the ladies were in the powder room, about fifteen minutes before the little hand and big hand had a meeting at the twelve. "Share the dedication with the girls, Joey. C'mon, you shithead!"

Joey was not the showboat type, lacking even a modicum of bravado in his makeup. He was in fact a little embarrassed to take out the paper that revealed the book dedication.

Never usually one to pass on an opportunity for the limelight,

Lou interjected, "I'd read it for you, buddy, but this is your show."

Joey rose from his chair and appeared uncomfortable as he fumbled for the handwritten paper that contained the words that had been carefully selected for his first venture into a bound publication. His years as a prominent sportswriter for the *New York Daily News*, writing his column, Sports Chat, had never included such a heartfelt prelude.

Joey, emboldened by the glowing smile of Susan, began,

"To Mom, Dad, and sis, thank you. To my wife, Susan, who has always stood by me, I love you, babe. Lastly, to my friends Bob and Lou, my brothers, without whom there would be no book, whenever you need me, I'll be there."

2

As Joey was being hugged by his wife, Susan, followed by Janet and Grace, Lou walked off with Bob.

"Bob, why don't you get drinks for everyone? I have to give my parents a buzz, they'll be expecting their 'Happy New Year' phone call."

"Sure thing, Fredo" is Bob's attempt to be clever by substituting Lou's name for the less-than-mentally-astute middle brother from *The Godfather*.

As Lou walked toward the phone booths, his smirking rebuttal is "Fuck you, Luca," a reference to Luca Brasi, a second brain-challenged character from the erstwhile Academy Award–winning film.

Lou dialed his parents. His mom was ecstatic when she heard her son's voice. "Alfredo, it's Lou." His dad was equally pleased that his younger son paid his wife and himself the respect of a phone call on New Year's Eve. "Happy New Year, son, we just got off the phone with your brother. He beat you this year."

"I'll call John in the morning, Dad. I love you guys."

Respect for his mom and dad, and for his entire family for that matter, was high in the pecking order for Lou Marciano. It came naturally since he was brought up that way. His friends, Joey and Bob, always cracked up at one of the favorite expressions of Lou's father: "Family first, bullshit second."

After Lou hung up the phone and walked to the bar, Bob was just about ready to take the drinks back to the table. He was conversing with the bartender, whom both he and Lou knew from their Monsignor McClancy High School baseball team.

On seeing Lou, the bartender and former teammate greeted him. "Hey, Marciano, how are you? Long time."

"Ralph? What the hell are you doing here?"

"What can I tell I tell you, Lou? I am doing OK. Working with the NYPD and usually do this gig one day a week. I have been married for five years, but no kids yet."

"Ralphie Boy, how about a joke for old time's sake?"

"For you, Lou, no problem."

Ralph took care of another patron's drink request and then began. "I was on a plane last week flying from Las Vegas to New York and we experienced significant turbulence. The pilot advised us of the conditions and identified that we would get through it in about 10 minutes. Anyway, after successfully piloting the plane through the turbulence the pilot, who had unintentionally left the intercom on, was heard saying to the co-pilot, 'damn, that was some rough shit, a blow job and a cup of coffee would hit the spot about now.' Hearing the obvious oversight by the pilot of leaving the intercom on for all to hear, a stewardess hurriedly made her way to the cockpit. As she passed by me, I uttered, 'don't forget the coffee!'"

As the three shared a laugh and continued to reminisce, up to the bar strode a Yankee favorite of Lou's. He recognized him immediately.

"Joe Pepitone! I have a baseball you autographed for my dad when you were in your rookie season."

Pepitone was his gregarious self and, at the behest of Lou, told one of his favorite Mickey Mantle stories. "We were set to play our annual exhibition game at West Point in 1968. Well, I was divorced at the time and was living at the St. Moritz Hotel in Manhattan with Mickey. It was Mickey's last year. Anyway, the team bus was scheduled to leave at nine thirty in the morning. Of course me and Mickey had gone out the night before, got plastered, and missed the freakin' bus. We each thought the other had requested a wake-up call."

Lou was cognizant of Pepitone's close relationship with his childhood idol. "You really looked up to the Mick, didn't you, Joe?"

"You got that right. He was not only the greatest ballplayer I ever saw, at least those first two years I was there, but I admired how the fuck the guy could play ball every day with his legs taped up like a mummy. And damn, he knew how to have a good time. But what I remember most is how he accepted me as a rookie in 1963 even though I had taken the place of his good friend Moose Skowron."

Bob awaited the completion of the story.

"Hey, Fredo, let Joe finish his story, would ya?"

Pepitone continued. "I tell Mickey that my car had been repossessed so he called for a limousine. I heard him on the phone demanding to speak to the driver. Then he requested that the guy bring along a gallon picnic jug filled with ice, a couple of quarts of vodka, and orange juice. Needless to say, by the time we arrived at West Point, we were even more bombed than we were when we had gotten in the night before."

Lou couldn't resist. "Joe, I just might like this story as much as the Phil Linz episode on the team bus when he was playing his harmonica. I think it was 'Mary Had a Little Lamb.' Yogi was yelling for quiet."

"Oh sure," interposed Pepitone. "That was when Yogi was the manager. Phil asked Mickey what Yogi had said, and Mickey told him that he wanted him to play it louder."

At this point, a dozen or so sports lovers gathered around Pepitone, and the showman basked in the acclamation.

"C'mon, Joe, finish the Mickey story at West Point" is Bob Murphy's request. Although an avid Willie Mays aficionado, Bob Murphy was a student of the game and recognized the true greatness of the Yankee, who, along with Willie and Duke, provided New York sports fans with an array of unparalleled center field talent in the fifties. He now clamored for the conclusion of the yarn.

Pepitone continued his anecdote. "As we approached the West Point Stadium field, the driver asked where we want to be dropped off. Mickey told him to pull up right onto the ball field. Of course, he could hardly be understood, so the driver asked again. Mickey became belligerent. 'You heard me, dickface, I said right on the fuckin' field.' Our teammates were all hysterical when they see the 25' Cadillac limo maneuver onto the baseball diamond. I had the window open and waved my baseball cap. Even Ralph Houk, our manager that year, couldn't help but crack up. Of course, it got totally out of control when Mickey stepped out of the car and fell right on his face."

As Pepitone was signing autographs, Bob and Lou headed back with the drinks.

Joey was upset when he heard that he had missed Joe Pepitone.

"I am going up to the bar, guys. I want to talk with him."

After a few minutes he returned with the identification that he has scheduled a meeting with Pepitone to discuss the first baseman/outfielder Yankee experiences. "He was a power hitter who could really pick it at first base. He won a few Gold Gloves at that position."

A Sports Chat article on the flamboyant kid from Brooklyn, who many felt never reached his full potential, appeared to be on the Joey Kowalski agenda.

Susan and Joey left the gala a little after 1:00 a.m. but not before dancing to one of their favorite new songs, the Bee Gees hit "How Deep Is Your Love."

The remaining two couples lit up the dance floor to several current hits, including Travolta and Newton-John's top-of-the-chart song from *Grease*, "You're the One That I Want," and Donna Summer's "Let's Dance." Then in the "who can hold his girlfriend closer" contest, with both his hands on her ass of course, slow dancing to the Righteous Brothers' "Unchained Melody."

The four had come in one car, all expecting to stay over that evening at Grace's house in Douglaston. Despite the protestations of Janet, Bob insisted that he was fine and drove. Lou sat in the back with Grace, and his torpor regarding speech was quite uncharacteristic.

Grace inquired, "Lou, you haven't said a word in five minutes. I thought you had fallen asleep. What are you thinking about, honey?"

Bob's laughter was irrepressible. "Yeah, Fredo, what the hell are you thinking about?"

"Out with it, Lou," said the front seat lovely, Janet. "What are you keeping from us, Mr. Marciano?"

"Well, I was thinking about what is more important in life, family or friends? I certainly love my family, but I don't know what the hell I would do without you guys."

"Go back to sleep, Marciano, you think too much" is Bob's chortling retort.

Grace had a temporary solution to the impasse facing her husband-to-be. "Why don't you prepare yourself for when we get home, Lou? You better not have had too much to drink, Mr. Italian Stallion!"

3

From a sports world perspective, 1979 would commence in an extraordinary manner for Joey Kowalski. It would be his first year as a Baseball Writers Association of America (BBWAA) member, to be eligible to cast a vote for the Hall of Fame. Joe, the first-name moniker he used professionally, was truly honored to have the privilege; hubris was not the least bit evident.

The process for voting had been modified in 1967. Each BBWAA member with ten or more years of service could select up to ten players who had been in the Major Leagues for a minimum of ten seasons and were out of baseball for at least five years. To be elected, a player was required to have his name be on a minimum of 75 percent of all ballots cast.

Joey had been a little deceptive with his buddies, not revealing that he would be casting his first ever vote for a players potential enshrinement in Cooperstown. The noted sports columnist felt it was incumbent that he studiously prepare for his first attempt at selecting the right candidates for the hallowed Hall of Fame.

On the initial Sunday of January, Bob and Lou came over to Joey and Susan's to watch the NFL championship games. It would be a football afternoon and their future spouses didn't care. Janet and Grace joined their beaus for the get-together but, in lieu of watching the pigskin broadcasts, would be reinforcing their indomitable friendship with Susan, who was approaching the seventh month of her pregnancy.

Bob and Lou had wagered with a mutual bookie friend on each game. Both had selected the Steelers, laying seven points against the Houston Oilers, and the Cowboys, a 3½-point favorite over the Rams.

"How much did you guys bet on each game?" Joey questioned.

Bob was quick to offer the answer. "Five hundred dollars on each game, we split it."

Lou had only one concern. "I hate betting on the fuckin' Cowboys. I think they'll cover, but it won't be as easy as Pittsburgh putting a hurtin' on Houston."

Joey, not inclined to jeopardize his good standing with the *New York Daily News* as their leading sportswriter, refrained from wagering but offered his commentary nonetheless. "The Steelers have to contain the beast." This was a reference to the Oilers' Earl Campbell, a combination of power and speed, reminiscent of the guy considered by most professional football experts to be the greatest running back of all time, Jim Brown.

Six hours of football later, Bob and Lou were gloating at their pigskin prognostication abilities.

- AFC championship
  Pittsburgh Steelers 34 – Houston Oilers 5
- NFC championship
  Dallas Cowboys 28 – Los Angeles Rams 0

"I like Bradshaw over Staubach in the Super Bowl," echoed Lou. Bob and Joey concurred.

This was Bob Murphy's rejoinder: "The Giants better get a QB who has the capability to take us to the next level in the draft this year." Bob was referring to the NFL Team of choice for all three, the New York Giants.

Lou has only one thought on his mind. "Yeah, and maybe we can get a guy who can be taught to take an effin' knee at the end of a game which we have in the bag."

His indication of disgust was over the disaster in the Meadowlands two months prior, when QB Joe Pisarcik and FB Larry Csonka failed to connect on an unnecessary handoff in lieu of a simple acceptance of the snap from center by the QB, followed by an undemanding placement of a knee on the turf.

"Unbelievable, just un-fuckin'-believable."

4

As the three couples were partaking in the desserts brought by the guests—a polish cheese bobka from Janet and Bob's favorite bakery and a homemade Italian cheesecake, a specialty of Grace, prepared with just a modicum of assistance from Lou—Joey casually had a revelation. He would be a first-time Hall of Fame voter and would be required to submit his ballot in a week. Joey hoped that, with the girls present, his identification would cause less of a conniption from either of his good pals. He was very, very mistaken. Two invective responses followed.

"What's that, Kowalski? You have a freakin' vote for the Hall this year and didn't tell us?" Bob was incensed.

"How would you know who the hell to vote for without talking to us, Joey? You have got to be kidding me, you kielbasa-lovin' asshole."

Lou Marciano could not believe that Joey had shunned him and Bob. He thought to himself, *How could he have even considered making his selections without them?*

Thirty minutes later, with the assistance of his wife, Susan, and Grace and Janet, Joey convinced his bosom buddies that making the selections for the Hall of Fame on his own was the appropriate thing to do.

"I believe in my heart that as a voter I have an obligation to do it without input from you guys."

Joey wanted to mitigate his apparent misstep and sought impunity. "How about we meet at Budd's next Friday night and I tell you how I went about reviewing the potential candidates and the history of recent Hall of Fame elections?"

Budd's was a Jackson Heights hangout for the guys ever since they had turned eighteen and were allowed to legally partake in firewater and the like.

"Here, you guys." Joey handed each of his friends a copy of the summary sheet he had prepared to assist himself with the selection of the top 1979 candidates for induction into the Hall. The chart was certainly an indication of Joey Kowalski being anything but hidebound in his analysis.

"You guys can digest this sheet before we meet. It is self- explanatory. Just refer to the notes." His quagmire was apparently surmounted.

Bob and Lou can't wait and are now concentrating on reviewing the handout. Their allegations of Joey's deceit in the "why didn't you tell us you had a vote" scandal were all but forgotten.

Murphy was emphatic. "You did this yourself, Kowalski? You actually only had to know one thing. It's Willie's first year of eligibility. Just write his name in ten times out of respect and be done with it." Willie Mays remained Bob's all-time favorite ballplayer.

Lou commends his sportswriter/author buddy, gesticulating like a true Italian. "Pretty impressive, Joey. I know for a fact that there are two guys on this summary sheet who will be included in your selections, Duke and Gil. Tell me no!"

His reference, of course, was to the Brooklyn Dodger idols of Joey's youth, Duke Snider and Gil Hodges.

As they were leaving Budd's, Lou offered a parting joke. "Did you guys hear that Mickey and Minnie Mouse are seeing a marriage counselor?

At their last meeting the counselor questions why Mickey is so upset about his wife being silly. Mickey responds with, 'I didn't say she was silly, I said she was fuckin' Goofy.'"

HALL OF FAME VOTING SUMMARY 1969 - 1978

TOP CANDIDATES	% OF VOTE									
	1969	1970	1971	1972	1973	1974	1975	1976	1977	1978
STAN MUSIAL	93.2 - (1)									
ROY CAMPANELLA	79.4 - (5)									
LOU BOUDREAUX	64.1 - (9)	77.3 - (10)								
RALPH KINER	40.3 - (7)	55.7 - (8)	58.9 - (9)	59.3 - (10)	61.8 - (11)	58.9 - (12)	75.4 - (13)			
ENOS SLAUGHTER	37.6 - (4)	44.3 - (5)	45.9 - (6)	37.6 - (7)	38.2 - (8)	39.7 - (9)	46.9 - (10)	50.8 - (11)	58.0 - (12)	68.9 - (13)
RED SCHOENDIENST	19.1 - (1)	32.3 (2)	34.2 - (3)	26.3 - (4)	25.3 - (5)	30.1 - (6)	26.0 - (7)	33.2 - (8)	27.4 - (9)	34.3 - (10)
EARLY WYNN	27.9 - (1)	46.7 - (2)	66.7 - (3)	76.0 - (4)						
PEE WEE REESE	26.2 - (5)	32.3 - (6)	35.3 -(7)	32.6 - (8)	33.2 - (9)	38.6 - (10)	42.5 - (11)	47.9 - (12)	42.6 - (13)	44.6 - (14)
GIL HODGES	24.1 - (1)	48.3 -(2)	50.0 - (3)	40.7 - (4)	57.4 - (5)	54.2 - (6)	51.9 - (7)	60.1 - (8)	58.5 - (9)	59.6 - (10)
PHIL RIZZUTO	22.9 -(7)	26.3 - (8)	25.6 - (9)	26.0 - (10)	29.2 - (11)	30.4 - (12)	32.3 - (13)	38.4 - (14)		
BOB LEMON	16.5 - (5)	25.0 - (6)	25.0 -(7)	29.5 - (8)	46.6 - (9)	52.1 - (10)	64.4 - (11)	78.6 - (12)		
RICHIE ASHBURN	2.9 - (2)	3.7 - (3)	2.8 - (4)	2.8 - (5)	8.6 - (6)	15.3 - (7)	32.0 - (8)	21.9 - (9)	36.3 - (10)	41.7 - (11)
DUKE SNIDER		17.0 - (1)	24.7 -(2)	21.2 - (3)	26.6 - (4)	30.4 - (5)	35.6 - (6)	41.0 - (7)	55.4 - (8)	67.0 - (9)
YOGI BERRA			67.2 - (1)	85.6 - (2)						
NELLIE FOX			10.8 - (1)	16.2 - (2)	19.2 - (3)	21.6 - (4)	21.0 - (5)	44.8 - (6)	39.7 - (7)	39.3 - (8)
SANDY KOUFAX				86.9 - (1)						
WARREN SPAHN					83.2 - (1)					
WHITEY FORD					67.1 - (1)	77.8 - (2)				
ROBIN ROBERTS					56.1 - (1)	61.4 - (2)	72.7 -(3)	86.9 - (4)		
MICKEY MANTLE						88.2 - (1)				
EDDIE MATHEWS						32.3 - (1)	40.9 - (2)	48.7 - (3)	62.4 - (4)	79.4 - (5)
ROGER MARIS						21.4 - (1)	19.3 - (2)	22.4 -(3)	21.4 - (4)	21.9 - (5)
DON DRYSDALE							21.0 - (1)	29.4 - (2)	51.4 - (3)	57.8 - (4)
ERNIE BANKS									83.8 - (1)	
JIM BUNNING									38.1 - (1)	47.8 - (2)
HOYT WILHELM										41.7 - (1)
MAURY WILLS										30.3 - (1)
WILLIE MAYS								BECOMES ELIGIBLE IN 1979		
LUIS APARICIO								BECOMES ELIGIBLE IN 1979		
# OF VOTERS	340	300	360	306	380	365	362	388	383	379

NOTES: 1. NUMBER IN BOXES REFLECT THE % OF VOTE TO THE LEFT AND THE # OF YEARS ON ON THE BALLOT TO THE RIGHT.
2. 75% OF THE VOTE REQUIRED FOR HALL OF FAME INDUCTION - ELECTED PLAYERS HIGHLIGHTED.

COMPILED BY JOE KOWALSKI DEC. 1978

5

The guys convened again at Budd's the following Friday at 8:00 p.m. Their hangout since the summer of 1962 was an establishment fraught with pleasant memories. Joey Kowalski's first book, *Dopey Bastid*, was often reviewed by Bob Murphy and Lou Marciano there; now they would offer their robust, unique, and yet insightful perspectives on Joey's Hall of Fame ballot for 1979.

The "Hall of Fame Voting Summary 1969–1978" sheet prepared by Joey was the initial topic of discussion. His clandestine attempt to conceal his voting intentions was no longer a topic of discussion.

"Kowalski, how can I ever call you a dopey bastard when you produced such a comprehensive masterpiece on the Hall of Fame? Great job, Joey."

Bob Murphy seconded the comments of Lou Marciano. "Yeah, Joey, it was pretty special. Now who did you put on your ballot after you wrote down Willie's name?"

Before the "who Joey anticipated voting for" discussion, the three brother-like pals discussed the peculiarities and highlights of the summary sheet.

- Fourteen players had been enshrined in Cooperstown over the prior ten years, namely the following:
  1. Stan Musial–St. Louis Cardinals (OF/1B, 1969)
  2. Roy Campanella–Brooklyn Dodgers (C, 1969)
  3. Lou Boudreaux–Cleveland Indians (SS,1970)

4. Sandy Koufax–Brooklyn/LA Dodgers (P, 1972)
5. Yogi Berra–New York Yankees (C, 1972)
6. Early Wynn–Cleveland Indians (P, 1972)
7. Warren Spahn–Milwaukee Braves (P, 1973)
8. Mickey Mantle–New York Yankees (OF, 1974)
9. Whitey Ford–New York Yankees (P, 1974)
10. Ralph Kiner–Pittsburgh Pirates (OF, 1975)
11. Robin Roberts–Philadelphia Phillies (P, 1976)
12. Bob Lemon–Cleveland Indians (P, 1976)
13. Ernie Banks–Chicago Cubs (SS/1B, 1977)
14. Eddie Mathews–Milwaukee Braves (3B, 1978)

- Of the fourteen, only five were selected in their first year of eligibility: Stan Musial, Sandy Koufax, Warren Spahn, Mickey Mantle, and Ernie Banks.
- It took three players ten or more years to achieve the required 75 percent vote: Lou Boudreaux, Ralph Kiner, and Bob Lemon.
- New York City SS stalwarts, Phil Rizzuto and Pee Wee Reese, both failed to be elected within fifteen years of retirement and were therefore no longer eligible to be voted by the baseball writers. Their fate would now be in the hands of the Veterans Committee.
- Enos Slaughter had one year of eligibility remaining. He had come extremely close in 1978, garnering 68.9 percent of the votes cast.
- Joey Kowalski's childhood idol, Duke Snider, in his ninth year on the ballot, had risen to a 67.0 percent level in 1978. Amazingly, in 1970, Snider's first eligible year, the Duke of Flatbush had only enticed a mere 17 percent of the writers to pen his name on their confidential submission.
- Joey was also quick to point out that he also had trouble reconciling the fact that his dad's favorite Brooklyn Dodger, Gil Hodges, had never reached the 75 percent plateau after ten years. Hodges had, however, broken the 50 percent

barrier for the sixth consecutive voting year in 1978 but remained 15 percent below the "promised land."

The primary candidates for 1979 election, based on the writers' prior year voting, were as follows: Enos Slaughter, Red Schoendienst, Gil Hodges, Richie Ashburn, Duke Snider, Nellie Fox, Roger Maris, Don Drysdale, Jim Bunning, Hoyt Wilhelm, and Maury Wills, all previously on the ballot and remaining eligible.

There were two prominent newcomers to the process, Willie Mays and Luis Aparicio. Mays was a no-brainer. Aparicio, an all-star shortstop predominantly for the White Sox and Orioles, was an excellent leadoff guy, slick with the glove and a prolific base stealer.

Lou offered his thoughts on both the summary sheet and his own 1979 selections.

"How can a number of your baseball writer brethren be so freakin' stupid? Maybe some just think that they can play God with their votes, because how could certain supposed experts not vote for Musial, Koufax, Spahn, Mickey [reference to Mantle, his childhood idol], and Banks in their first year of eligibility. Shit, Yogi [Berra] shouldn't have had to wait until his second year to get in. The only player with over 90 percent of the vote of those six no-doubters was Stan the Man. I also did some quick research during the week. Would you believe that Joe DiMaggio only got 44.3 percent of the vote in 1953, then 69.4 percent in 1954, before climbing to 88.8 percent in 1955? Joey, if you write a sequel to your book, you have the first bunch of dopey bastards from the BBWAA. Listen, I didn't even mention the Duke. What a disgrace that your guy isn't in yet."

After a second round of beers was ordered, Lou continued.

"There is no way I'd ever vote for Schoendienst. That pecker fell on Mickey's right shoulder on a play at second base in the '58 World Series. That impaired his throwing ability. OK, I got that off my chest so here goes. If I had a vote, I would start with Willie and Duke, include two more Dodgers, Hodges and Drysdale, and then add a guy who was a great all- around player, won back-to-back MVPs, and just happened to beat the Babe's HR record. Roger [Maris] deserves to be in. I would leave it at that for this year, five guys."

Bob was still incredulous regarding Lou's revelation of one of baseball's all-time greats. "My God, Lou, Joe D. didn't get into the Hall until his third year of eligibility?" Bob Murphy was a New York Giant fan when baseball ruled the streets of New York's five boroughs. Willie Mays was his guy. Yet he understood and respected the greatness of the three other center fielders that graced the outfield grass at either Yankee Stadium or Ebbets Field, while Willie patrolled the spacious Polo Grounds for his Giants. He was cognizant of the fact that Joe DiMaggio was the predecessor to and paved the way for Willie, Mickey, and the Duke.

Bob continued. "As I was saying, that is fuckin' disgraceful about DiMaggio, and Duke certainly deserved to get in a long time ago. All I can add is, how could you ever leave Willie's name off of your ballot this year? That said, besides the 'greatest of all time,' I would add Duke and Hodges and that's it. I think three guys are enough to vote for in any given year."

Lou needled his good buddy. "Mickey is already in, why would you vote for him?"

This was his way of acknowledging that the "greatest of all time" statement referred to his childhood idol, Mantle, and not to Bob's all-time baseball favorite, Willie Mays.

"Screw you, Marciano, you know who I was talking about."

Joey was pleased that Lou and Bob had provided their input. His thinking for enshrinement was vitalized by their comments.

"Well, my good friends, I guess it is time that I reveal my voting decision. I am pretty much in concert with both of your thinking.

My ballot will include, in this order, Mays, Snider, Hodges, Drysdale, Kluszewski, and Mazeroski. The latter two guys I just had to add since I felt that there should be more Polacks in Cooperstown. Plus Mazeroski hit the home run, which caused Marciano to cry like a baby."

"Get the hell out of here, Kowalski, you didn't include Big Klu [Kluszewski] or that shithead Mazeroski, did you?" Lou looked for Joey to recant.

Bob was sure that Joey was just trying his best to get a reaction from his cronies. "Maybe he did include those two guys, Lou. He's probably the only sportswriter who knows how to spell their names. Joey probably can't wait for Yastrzemski to be eligible."

In fact, Joey had only the first four names on his list.

Less than two weeks later, after Terry Bradshaw had thrown four touchdown passes in leading the Pittsburgh Steelers over the Dallas Cowboys 35–31 in Super Bowl XIII, the vote was published.

Willie Mays at 94.7 percent was the sole selectee. Much to the chagrin of Joey, Duke fell just short at 71.3 percent, followed by Enos Slaughter at 68.8 percent, Hodges at 56.0 percent, and Drysdale at 53.9 percent. Lou's push for Roger Maris was not heeded by many as only 127 of the 432 votes cast included the regular season home run king.

The following Sports Chat column of Joey Kowalski appeared in the *New York Daily News* after the Hall of Fame voting.

Sports Chat by Joe Kowalski
January 24, 1979

Congratulations, Willie. The enshrinement of number 24 was never in doubt. That said, as a first-time voter for the hollowed Cooperstown induction, I must say that I am disappointed in many of my fellow journalists.

Gil Hodges and Duke Snider belong in the Hall of Fame; there should be no doubt.

Gil Hodges was one of the best fielding first baseman of all time. His dexterity with the glove combined with the following hitting stats should convince you he belongs. Would you believe that Hodges led the Major Leagues in RBIs in the decade of the fifties? How about the fact that at the time of his retirement Gil was the all-time leading right-handed HR hitter in the National League? C'mon guys, what the hell are you thinking?

Now, let me commiserate about my childhood hero, Edwin "Duke" Snider. When I was in the eighth grade, my two best friends and I wrote a book report on our favorite players: Willie Mays, Mickey Mantle, and Duke Snider. It was the fall of 1957. Our account compared the three during the 1951 through 1957 seasons, the years that those center field icons played in New York City at the same time. Willie and Mickey were rookies in 1951, and Duke had been around since 1947. To be totally factual, Willie and Duke played the middle outfield position for the Giants and Dodgers respectively in '51. Mickey was in right field his first year; the great Joe DiMaggio still patrolled center field in the Bronx, his last year in the big leagues. Well, I digress.

There are two things for me to show you. The first is the summary stat sheet that appeared in our report. Here it is.

	GAMES	PA	AB	HITS	BA	HR	HR/AB	WALKS	TB	OB%	SLUG %	OBS	RUNS	R/PA	RBI'S	RBI/AB
SNIDER																
1951	150	672	606	168	0.277	29	4.8%	82	293	0.344	0.483	0.827	96	0.143	101	0.167
1952	141	598	534	162	0.303	21	3.9%	59	264	0.368	0.494	0.862	80	0.134	92	0.172
1953	151	660	590	198	0.336	42	7.1%	82	370	0.419	0.627	1.046	132	0.194	126	0.214
1954	149	679	584	199	0.341	40	6.9%	84	378	0.423	0.647	1.070	120	0.177	130	0.223
1955	148	653	538	166	0.309	42	7.8%	104	338	0.418	0.628	1.046	126	0.193	136	0.253
1956	150	652	542	158	0.292	43	7.9%	99	324	0.399	0.598	0.997	112	0.172	101	0.186
1957	139	592	508	139	0.274	40	7.9%	77	293	0.366	0.587	0.955	91	0.154	92	0.181
TOTALS	1022	4526	3902	1190	0.305	257	6.6%	567	2265	0.395	0.580	0.975	757	0.167	778	0.199
MAYS																
1951	121	524	464	127	0.274	20	4.3%	57	219	0.356	0.472	0.828	59	0.113	68	0.147
1952	34	144	127	30	0.236	4	3.1%	16	52	0.326	0.409	0.735	17	0.118	23	0.181
1953				IN MILITARY SERVICE												
1954	151	640	565	195	0.345	41	7.3%	66	377	0.411	0.667	1.078	119	0.186	110	0.195
1955	152	670	580	185	0.319	51	8.8%	79	382	0.400	0.659	1.059	123	0.184	127	0.219
1956	152	650	578	171	0.296	36	6.2%	68	322	0.369	0.557	0.926	101	0.155	84	0.145
1957	152	688	585	195	0.333	35	6.0%	78	386	0.427	0.626	1.033	112	0.168	97	0.166
TOTALS	762	3296	2899	903	0.311	187	6.5%	362	1718	0.390	0.593	0.983	531	0.161	509	0.176
MANTLE																
1951	96	386	341	91	0.267	13	3.8%	43	151	0.349	0.443	0.792	61	0.158	65	0.191
1952	142	626	549	171	0.311	23	4.2%	75	291	0.394	0.530	0.924	94	0.150	87	0.158
1953	127	540	461	136	0.295	21	4.6%	79	229	0.368	0.497	0.895	105	0.194	92	0.200
1954	145	651	543	163	0.300	27	5.0%	102	285	0.408	0.525	0.933	129	0.198	102	0.188
1955	147	638	517	158	0.306	37	7.2%	113	316	0.431	0.611	1.042	121	0.190	99	0.191
1956	150	652	533	188	0.353	52	9.8%	112	376	0.464	0.705	1.169	132	0.202	130	0.244
1957	144	623	474	173	0.365	34	7.2%	146	315	0.512	0.665	1.177	121	0.194	94	0.195
TOTALS	952	4116	3418	1080	0.316	207	6.1%	670	1963	0.429	0.574	1.003	763	0.185	669	0.196

This synopsis is certainly indicative of the veracity of my guy, Duke, for Hall of Fame induction. Yet sometimes stats don't tell the whole story. How about listening to what Snider meant to a thirteen-year-old Brooklyn Dodger fan in 1957. In that regard, I would like you to read what I had written twenty-one years ago as my conclusion to the book report. By the way, it was a joint decision for each of us to write our own finale to our commentary. The other two guys—we were and still remain best friends, you know—wrote about Willie and Mickey. It was the best way to wrap up our report. So here is my conclusion in 1957. Just for the record, the Joey Kowalski thoughts on the Duke of Flatbush haven't changed.

"Duke Snider, the Duke of Flatbush, has been my baseball hero since I was six years old. My dad, my sister, and I often drove the twelve miles from Queens to Brooklyn to watch the Dodgers play at Ebbets Field. It was continually an extraordinary experience. We always sat in the right center field bleachers, as far to right field as possible. My dad knew that my biggest thrill would be to catch a home run ball hit by Duke. I brought along my Duke Snider mitt and actually came close once. Too bad there had been a real tall guy in front of me in July 1955. I know I would have made the catch of that Duke blast.

"Anyhow, October of that year was the best time of my life. Watching and listening to the World Series in 1955 and just looking at the expressions on my sister's and dad's faces when our Dodgers beat the Yankees in game 7 to win their first World Series championship are something I will never forget. And the catalyst for my happiness was Duke Snider.

"He was simply the best ballplayer on a great team. Watching him play center field, particularly after making a great catch or throw, was the best tonic for any day I didn't feel well or was full of anxiety due to an impending exam at school. The beauty of his left-handed swing was also something to behold. The most feared hitter in the National League was a statement I read often in the Daily News, the Daily Mirror, and the Herald Tribune. Sorry about that, Sister (let me clarify here—I was speaking of Sister Marie Angela, my eighth-grade teacher at St. Joan of Arc grammar school). Maybe Stan the Man (Stan Musial, her favorite player) was just past his prime.

"So now what? Duke is moving to Los Angeles. I feel like I'm losing one of my best friends. No offense, Bob and Lou. I just hope that Duke continues his fantastic string of hitting over forty home runs in five consecutive seasons. I dream about maybe having my dad take me down to Philadelphia to see him play there next season.

Thank you, Duke, for being there for me. You are the best center fielder in New York. Hope to see you again soon."

The exodus to the West Coast of the Brooklyn Dodgers and New York Giants after the 1957 season left a bevy of their fans longing to see the great center fielders from their respective teams. Duke Snider (left) and Willie Mays were perennial all-stars and two-thirds of the sacred New York trilogy—Willie, Mickey, and the Duke. Snider was not as dominant in Los Angeles, however, while Mays continued to flourish and display his five tool skills in San Francisco. Mays was a first ballot Hall of Famer in 1979. Snider remarkably was below the 75 percent induction requirement until his eleventh year of eligibility in 1980.

Pictured above from left to right are Roger Maris, Yogi Berra, and Mickey Mantle. The iconic Mantle was a first- ballot Hall of Famer. Berra, one of the greatest catchers in baseball history and a three-time MVP winner, was deprived of induction until his second year of eligibility. Maris, a back-to-back MVP winner in 1960 and 1961, the year he eclipsed the Babe Ruth single season HR record of 60 by one home run, never achieved enough votes for induction. Nonsupporters would allude to his less than stellar .260 lifetime batting average.

CHAPTER II

MAGIC AND BIRD

1

The Pittsburgh Steelers Super Bowl XIII victory over the Cowboys had left both Bob and Lou in an extremely favorable mood—the result of another five-hundred- dollar profit for each after wagering correctly, albeit "stepping in it," laying 3½ points, and winning by 4. They decided to treat Susan and Joey, along with their brides- to-be, to dinner at Luigi's, the favorite restaurant of the dirty half dozen. "We'll split the bill, Marciano," offered Robert Murphy to his successful betting companion.

The conversation for that Sunday afternoon centered around Susan Kowalski's impending motherhood and the dual wedding of Janet and Bob and Grace and Lou, now tentatively scheduled eight months in the future. This assumed that there would be no problem with the looming annulment of Janet's first marriage.

The lack of sports in the discussion was palpable.

"What a boring time of the year," observed Bob Murphy. "Football is over, the Knicks are playing like shit, the NCAA tournament is over a month down the road, and the baseball season is two months away."

Lou Marciano touted the Rangers. "Well, the Blueshirts beat the Islanders again last night. That's two in a row over those shitheads."

Joey couldn't leave well enough alone. "Yeah, Lou, but we lost to them in the first three games."

"Bite me, Kowalski," observes Lou, by no means oblique, as he beckoned, Carmella, Luigi's daughter, to the table. "Carmella, if Grace wasn't here, I'd ask you to run away with me."

Grace, always prepared to put her love interest in his place, simply shook her head. "If you want him, Carmella, you can have him."

Bob sought to put in his three cents. He was never just satisfied with two. "Forget about Lou, Carmella, you should be singing to me like Olivia Newton John sang to John Travolta, 'You're the one that I want.'" Bob momentarily paused. "Or would that be 'I'm the one that you want'?"

Janet now interjected, "Carmella can do a lot better than either of you egotistical buffoons."

Susan was hysterical, but her stomach was gurgling. "Can you order some appetizers, Lou, I'm starving."

Lou had known Luigi's family since he was a young child, and his uncle Vincent, aunt Helen, father, mother, and brother were frequent patrons.

"Anything for you, Mrs. Kowalski? Carmella, can you bring us some hot and cold trays family-style. You know, just like what your dad usually does for my family. These guys are my second family, so make it special."

Within ten minutes prosciutto, salami, provolone, sliced tomatoes with mozzarella, red peppers, assorted Italian olives, and artichoke hearts filled one platter, while the hot tray included eggplant parmigiana, stuffed mushrooms, baked clams, mussels, shrimp, fried calamari, and fried zucchini. A large basket of sliced Italian bread with olive oil complimented the premeal feast.

Joey is in his glory. "My God, and this is just the prelim. Hey, Bob, remember when you and I used to go over to Lou's house earlier than he expected because we knew that his mom would be bringing us Sunday afternoon meal leftovers?"

"You got that right, Kowalski. We coined that the 'Marciano Sunday eatathons.'"

Lou smiled as he listened to the kind words about his mother, Rose Marciano, from Joey and Bob. He thought to himself, *Family and friends, who has it better than me?*

2

On March 9 the National Collegiate Athletic Association (NCAA) basketball tournament commenced. Joe Kowalski was one of the sportswriters assigned by the *New York Daily News* to follow the prestigious tournament in his Sports Chat column.

Forty teams vied for the national championship. The participants were divided into four brackets of ten teams, each ranked by the NCAA Committee based on record, strength of schedule, and although no committee member would ever admit it, school reputation.

The top four seeds were as follows:

- East – North Carolina
- Mideast – Notre Dame
- Midwest – Indiana State
- West – UCLA

The six highest-ranked teams in each region were given a bye, as teams 7 through 10 played a first-round game. The winners of these eight contests joined the twenty-four nonplaying teams in the round of 32.

Bob Murphy had the biggest rooting interest of the trio of friends, having graduated from St. John's University in 1966 and receiving high acclaim as a center fielder on the baseball team. Bob was on Joey's case to write something favorable about the Redmen immediately after the tenth seed in the east advanced to the final thirty-two teams with a 75–70 first-round victory over Temple.

"Thata baby Louie," exclaimed Murphy. "Now let's send the Blue Devils home with tears in their eyes."

The first reference was not to his good friend Lou Marciano but rather to Lou Carnesecca, St. John's popular and entertaining coach; the latter, the nickname of St. John's second-round opponent, Duke.

Joey Kowalski and Lou Marciano were fully supportive of the Bob Murphy rooting interest. Their alumni affiliations at Columbia University and Manhattan College respectively left them both without a dog in the fight for the quest of the college basketball holy grail.

Murphy really began tooting his horn after the Redmen's two-point victory over the second-seeded Blue Devils advanced his alma mater into the round of 16, more popularly known as the Sweet Sixteen.

"I see final four on the horizon for my Johnnies."

The Lou Carnesecca–led squad did not disappoint Bob in their third contest as they defeated Rutgers, 67–65 and now were one win away from the Murphy prediction coming true. The University of Pennsylvania awaited them in the east final.

Bob was in an orgasmic state, a paradigm of optimism. "Don't tell Janet, but watching my boys pull out these wins is just as good as having sex."

"Well, since I have been cut off with Susan being due any day now, I'll stay on the St. John's bandwagon with you, my friend. You can forget about the 'being as good as sex' stuff though."

"Barbara and Terri must be working overtime, Kowalski."

"Who the hell are Barbara and Terri, Lou?"

"I thought that they were the names of your right hand and left hand."

3

Saturday, March 17, St. Patrick's Day—Joe Kowalski's Sports Chat column was read with admiration by his lifelong buddies. Bob, with perhaps a bit more curiosity, as an alumnus of St. John's.

Well, this year the NCAA tournament has not failed to entertain the lovers of the Naismith, "throw the ball into the peach basket" game. March Madness is in full swing and the Elite Eight has a plethora of intrigue to offer, especially for us New Yorkers.

The east final will pit one of our own, St. John's, piloted by their inimitable coach, Lou Carnesecca, versus the University of Pennsylvania, the ninth seed in the region. Little Louie, whose sweaters are the envy of many, will seek to eliminate the Quakers. It will be New York versus Philadelphia. Who could have forecast the two lowest seeds in the east playing in the regional championship?

Magic Johnson and the Michigan State Spartans have dismantled two opponents and will face Digger Phelps and the Irish of Notre Dame in the mideast final. I don't know whose face the TV cameras will be focused on more—the ever broad-smiling Magic or the former Fordham coach who gained local approbation of leading the Rams in the borough of the Bronx?

Indiana State, guided by the all-around performance of Larry Bird, remains undefeated on the season and will play Arkansas in the midwest final. Bird kinda reminds me of a larger version of Bill Bradley when he was leading his Princeton team in 1965—a dominant player on an otherwise team of unknowns. I am trying to figure out a way to get Bird on the Knicks, but as of now, the Celtics have his rights until this year's draft. Great move on their part selecting him with a future pick in the first round last year.

Finally, in the world of "what else is new" in college basketball, the Bruins of UCLA are in the west regional final and will take the hardwood against DePaul and their esteemed coach, Ray Meyer.

A quick note on UCLA is in order. Apologies to the likes of Adolph Rupp at Kentucky, but the Blue Demons are awaiting the team with the most dominant history in college basketball.

John Wooden, the former UCLA coach, respectfully coined as the Wizard of Westwood, set a standard of excellence that will in all likelihood never be surpassed. Take a peek at the last decade and a half. For you nonmathematicians, that span commences in 1964 and continues through last year.

- 1966 – Texas Western
- 1974 – North Carolina State
- 1976 – Indiana
- 1977 – Marquette
- 1978 – Kentucky

What about the ten missing years, you ask? Well, since 1964, there has been only one other school that has hoisted the trophy, which epitomizes college basketball supremacy—UCLA. To more emphatically state the case for Wooden and the Bruins, UCLA won the college basketball crown ten times in twelve years. Wooden retired after the 1975 championship season, so the last three years are added only to take us to this year's tournament.

Well, back to the 1979 college round ball pursuit. Although my prognostication prowess is not the equal to that of my two best friends, often referenced in this column, here are my predictions for the final four.

St. John's 72 – Penn 70

My heart is with Little Louie even though I really can't stand his sweaters. Also, my good friend Bob would kill me if I picked against the school for which he starred in center field, and Lou, you know the Yankee fan, my other best friend, likes St. John's as well.

In the mideast, I think that it will be the end of the line for Digger and the Irish. That kid Magic has much more than just a smile—a Bob Cousy-like guard who stands eight inches taller. I like the Spartan supporting cast also, particularly, Greg Kelser, their leading scorer. He is a star in his own right. I'll go with Michigan State 84 – Notre Dame 77.

Damn, I hope picking against the Irish on St. Patty's Day does not condemn me to hell.

Moving to the midwest region, you gotta like Larry Bird and his undefeated Indiana State Sycamores. I love the way Bird plays. He'll need help to lead his team over the Razorbacks from Arkansas, but I'll take them in a close one. Indiana State 78 – Arkansas 75.

John Wooden has been retired for over three years and I don't see Kareem Abdul-Jabaar (a.k.a. Lew Alcindor— he dominated high school basketball in the mid sixties in New York City at Power Memorial High School and in his years at UCLA) or Bill Walton on the court for the Bruins. Both my heart (because of Coach Ray Meyer) and my head tell me to go with the team from the windy city. How about DePaul 89 – UCLA 86?

So there you have the Joey Kowalski final four for this year: St. John's, Michigan State, Indiana State, and DePaul. Not bad, right? Two preeminent coaches, Lou Carnesecca and Ray Meyer from the east and west regions, and two players destined for greatness, Magic Johnson and Larry Bird.

Happy St. Patrick's Day, everyone. Can I have kielbasa instead of corned beef with my cabbage?

4

Later that day, at 7:11 p.m., Grace Janet Kowalski was born. It was in fact the best St. Patty's Day ever for Susan and Joey. The six-pound, thirteen-ounce infant, named after Susan's two best friends, couldn't wait until her end- of-March due date.

The parents of both Mom and Dad, their siblings, and of course the "just like sisters and brothers" Grace, Janet, Bob, and Lou were on hand.

Joey relayed the story of his Lamaze experience. "I was yelling 'push, push' and Susan is returning fire with 'get the hell out of here, sauerkraut breath.' The doctor and nurses were cracking up."

Once things were settled and all had been blessed with the view of Grace Janet's cherubic smile, it was time for Bob and Lou to take Joey for a celebration drink. The guys left their brides-to-be with Susan and the baby. There was no way that Grace and Janet were leaving Flushing Hospital until physically forced to vacate.

At Clancy's bar, Lou recalled what he had told Joey and Susan several months earlier, when the "Kowalski baby name" number game was played. This had resulted in an autograph of Robert Louis Kowalski, if the child were a boy.

"There was no freakin' way I wanted to see you have a boy, Kowalski. The kid would have grown up to be a pansy with a name like that. Thank God for baby girls."

"Fuck you, Marciano, the name Robert would have been great for the kid. Louis would have sucked but they could have just called the kid Bobby."

Bob Murphy had spoken and Joey and Lou just had no other recourse but irrepressible laughter.

"I think that this is the greatest day in my life, guys. I haven't been to church in over five years. St. Joan of Arc gets Joey Kowalski back tomorrow."

"Let's do another shot," said Lou.

As the three finished partaking in a jigger of Jameson's, the proud dad got a little antsy since he realized that his place was with Susan and his newborn daughter.

"C'mon, guys, let's get back to the hospital."

When they arrived back at Susan's bedside, they found her with Grace Janet in her arms and her sister-like girlfriends, Grace and Janet, begging to hold their "niece." Joey was certainly not opposed to this request but took his firstborn lovingly in his own arms. "First, Daddy, then your Aunt Grace and Aunt Janet."

Susan informed Joey that he missed both his and her parents and also his sister. "They all just left a few minutes ago. Your parents told me they would be back tomorrow. See that package on the window sill? Your mom said to take that home."

Joey felt sorry he had missed his family. Gently handing his daughter back to her mommy, he meandered over to see what was in the package left by his close-knit Polish family. Jackpot! Food would not be a concern for Joey or a strain on Susan when she was able to return home.

"What you got there, Kowalski?" inquired Lou.

Joey beamed at the immediate thoughtfulness of his family. Mom had come through big time. The package included many of his childhood eating favorites:

- golumkis—stuffed cabbage
- pierogis—two kinds of a Polish favorite type of fried dumplings; one filled with a mixture of sweet cheese and sauerkraut, and the other, mushrooms
- kielbasa—several large pieces of Polish sausage
- babka—Polish sweet yeast cake; once again, two kinds: cheese and chocolate

Lou recognized the expression on Joey's face when food earned his undivided attention. "Hey, Kowalski, you look as if you just pitched a no-hitter for McClancy [the high school in Queens attended by Joey, Bob, and Lou]. Listen, my mom is making you some of her specialties for me to bring over to you tomorrow."

Unbeknownst to his friends, on their return from the bar, Bob, claiming the male right to excrete the resultant fluids from the consumption of several beers, had noticed something special in the hospital gift shop and made a purchase. It was a large green teddy bear with a "Happy St. Patrick's Day" inscription.

Murphy walked over to Janet with the gift bag in hand and said, "Here, hot stuff, give this to our niece."

The gift for Grace Janet was warmly received. In addition to accolades from Susan, Joey, Grace, and Lou, the thoughtful and sincere present earned Bob a special treat under the blankets from Janet late that evening.

Susan had forgotten to share with Joey a package left by her mom and dad. It was to be opened only after Joey had returned. Her dad indicated that it was in the O'Connor family before coming to the US from Ireland prior to the turn of the century.

Joey found a knitted inscription covered with glass, in an unadorned wooden frame. His spouse requested that it be read and he obliged.

"A newborn babe brings light to the cottage, warmth to the heart, and joy to the soul. For wealth is family, family is wealth."

5

The following day everyone remained in a jovial mood, except for one Robert Murphy. St. John's succumbed to Penn, 64–62.

The final four would see the pairings of Penn versus Michigan State and Indiana State versus DePaul.

"Hey Bob, the *New York Daily News* columnist observed, if you hadn't coaxed me into rooting for the Redmen, I would have picked every team correctly."

"If it wasn't such a special time for you and Susan, Joey, I'd tell you to suck my big one."

"C'mon now, Bob, let's not exaggerate again," admonished Lou. "If that guppy between your legs is a 'big one,' then maybe you'd like me to pull down my zipper so that you can take a gander at Orca."

"Bite me, Marciano. Or should I just refer to you as Fredo, you shithead!"

Sports Chat by Joe Kowalski
March 26, 1979 (excerpt)

And then there were two. The 1979 championship final is set. Tonight's contest in Salt Lake City, Utah, pits the Michigan State Spartans, off of a rout of Penn 101-67, against undefeated Indiana State. The Sycamores margin of victory versus DePaul was a mere basket, 76–74. The two best players in college basketball, at least to many a sportswriter, commentator, or coach, will face off—Earvin "Magic" Johnson and Larry Bird. The debate of the experts is whether Bird can singlehandedly overcome Magic and his unquestionably stronger supporting cast, which includes a legitimate second star, forward, Greg Kelser. Michigan State versus Indiana State is destined to be the most watched college basketball game ever. Move over, Lew Alcindor and Elvin Hayes.

Magic and Bird dominated the headlines and pregame hype. Each at 6'9" in height and well proportioned, it was the sophomore, Johnson, facing the senior, Bird. Each star is a product of the state in which their school was situated—Magic from Lansing, Michigan, and Bird, the native of French Lick, Indiana.

After two years at Michigan State, the multifaceted Johnson averaged just over 17 points, 7.6 rebounds, and nearly 8 assists per game. His dexterity at the guard position was unheard of for an athlete of his height, an asset that afforded him tremendous court vision and the ability to make passes that a shorter player would have difficulty producing.

Larry Bird was primarily a scorer and rebounder for his team although his court IQ was acutely evident, and if an open man in scoring position were at hand, the ball would be at his fingertips in an instant. His three-year career averages for the Sycamores were 30.3 points, 13.3 rebounds, and 4.6 assists.

The three amigos were obviously together to view the contest. Joey had taken several days off after the birth of Grace Janet but returned to writing his column, Sports Chat. Fortunately, the championship game was being covered by another *Daily News* writer, and he therefore watched as a spectator with Bob and Lou.

Remarkably, neither Bob nor Lou had bet on the matchup. They had similar feelings regarding the game, each with a rooting interest for Indiana State to remain unbeaten but thinking that Michigan State would be too strong for the undefeated school with Larry Bird but not much of a supporting cast.

Joey was in the minority, agreeing with one of his favorite coaches of all time, Al Maguire of Marquette, who saw Indiana State as the eventual winner.

With a well-designed defensive zone scheme by Michigan State coach, Jud Heathcote, Bird was stifled. There was invariably a second defender available to limit the scoring prowess of the Indiana State star. The resultant 7 for 21 shooting and 19 overall points was more than offset by 24 points from Magic. The final score had the Big Ten powerhouse Michigan State as the 75–64 victor. Magic Johnson was named as the tournament's most outstanding player.

"Those two guys are going to be stars in the NBA for a long, long time," so said Bob Murphy.

"No shit, Einstein," Lou Marciano rebutted.

The sportswriter and novelist Joey Kowalski closed the conversation. "'Magic and Bird'—that has a nice ring to it."

It is not always a given that great collegiate basketball players achieve a similar status in the professional ranks. Perhaps the all-around skills on the hardwood, court savvy, and will to win made the transition seamless for Magic Johnson (left) and Larry Bird. The duo are pictured prior to the 1979 NCAA championship game, won by Magic's Michigan State Spartans over Bird's previously undefeated Sycamores of Indiana State. Magic and Bird continued one of the greatest rivalries in NBA history as they often faced off while playing for the Lakers and Celtics respectively. Each was a three-time NBA MVP.

CHAPTER III

UNSPECTACULAR BID

1

The spring of 1979 was active for the three couples, all of whom had grown up in Jackson Heights, Queens.

The new mom and dad prepared for the christening of Grace Janet. Susan and Joey had always been a model couple. Now it seemed as if the birth of their daughter had brought the relationship to another echelon.

Gradually, the sportswriter regained the attentiveness to his column which had garnered him accolades for several years.

Here is Joey's column which appeared on Kentucky Derby day. It was the Saturday after the NFL draft and the NHL playoff series between the New York Rangers and New York Islanders was in full swing.

Sports Chat by Joe Kowalski
May 5, 1979

It's a sports lover's delight in New York. Here are the three questions of the day. Can you believe that none of them are related to the boys in the Bronx or the group posing as ballplayers in Queens?

Will the two minutes of exhilaration today at Churchill Downs commence the legitimate pursuit of a third consecutive Triple Crown winner?

Has the NFL draft satisfactorily whet the appetites of Giant and Jet fans?

A hockey rivalry has evolved, which elicits fervor between the New York City traditionalists and the "new blood" Long Island contingent. Which local team will advance to play for the Stanley Cup?

Spectacular Bid will win the Derby; the two-year-old champion, who has added five more wins this year and remains undefeated, is far superior to the pack. Put your wallets and pocketbooks away, however. He'll only pay about three dollars on a two-dollar bet. Watch and enjoy for the sport of it. I have one very slight concern regarding the race outcome, the performance of teenage jockey, Ronnie Franklin. I don't see the poise of last year's youthful phenom, Steve Cauthen. I've heard rumblings that his trainer, Bud Delp, questions whether he should have sought a more seasoned rider for what could very well be the beginning of a Triple Crown trifecta, following Seattle Slew in 1977 and Affirmed last year.

The New York Giants, with the seventh pick in the NFL draft, sought to wash away years of frustration, and the bitter taste of the totally unnecessary Joe Pisarcik botched handoff to Larry Csonka last fall. Phil Simms, out of little known Morehead State, will endeavor to make Big Blue fans forget the likes of Charley Conerly, YA Title, and Fran Tarkenton. As for me, I am just hoping that he can win the starting job behind center and make me forget Gary Wood. To be totally forthright, I would have selected O. J. Anderson, the RB out of Miami (he was taken on the next pick by St. Louis) and looked to trade for a veteran as a stop gap measure. The QB crop will be more plentiful next year. Hey, Norm Sneed and Craig Morton fit the bill in that regard in the past. I may have waited to select a QB also. That kid from Notre Dame, Joe Montana, didn't get selected by the 49ers until the third round. Well, enough about the Giant first-round pick. I did like the addition of Earnest Gray with the second pick. He will make the receiving corps more formidable, and at least Simms will have a potential go-to guy to throw to.

The Jets made a solid pick at number 14 with the selection of Marty Lyons, the defensive end from Alabama. I seem to recall that they have had success drafting from that university in the past. The verdant and white will have the making of a solid defensive front when the rookie is added to the likes of Joe Klecko and Abdul Salaam. I'm not quite sure what the Jets were thinking when they took another defensive end, Mark Gastineau, with their second pick. I guess the Jet scouts know something I don't. He does have the reputation of being very athletic.

The New York Rangers and New York Islanders are certainly providing excitement for puck lovers. Can the Blueshirts win a cup for the first time since 1940? Will the Islanders, with a team who outscored their opponents in the regular season by an incredible 144 goals, win their first championship?

The Rangers disposed of the LA Kings and Philadelphia Flyers to reach the Stanley Cup semifinals, while the Islanders needed only to make the Chicago Black Hawk fans sob like babies with soiled diapers after their four- game sweep, thereby earning the right to face their archrivals from the Big Apple. (Just a side note for anyone interested in sports jerseys. The Black Hawks have the best in all sports. Take your pick of either the home or away uniform.)

The Islanders were the far superior team during the 1978– 1979 season, accumulating 116 points to the Rangers 91, and winning the head-to-head matchup five games to three. Their number one line of Trottier, Bossy, and Gillies was the best in hockey, accounting for an amazing 151 goals, 69 by Bossy. Dennis Potvin, their first team all-star defenseman, added 31 from the backline.

But in sports, the playoffs commence a new season, and that is especially true in the game played with the black one inch thick, three inches in diameter vulcanized rubber thingy. The Ranger coach, Fred Shero, has his team playing a solid brand of two-way hockey and John Davidson, with a not so impressive 3.52 goals against average during the regular season, has been stellar. In the four games that the teams have split, Big John has allowed only seven goals in regulation time to the high-powered Islander offense. Al Arbour, the bench leader for the Long Island squad, may have thought he had the edge in net with his tandem of Billy Smith and Glenn Resch, but that certainly has not been the case.

Well, the series is tied after the exciting OT win by the Islanders at the Garden on Thursday night, their second victory after the standard three twenty-minute periods.

In any event, hockey will be with us for a few more weeks since one of the two teams will reach the cup finals. My two good buddies are hoping that Davidson, Espo, and company can end the thirty-nine-year drought to bring Lord Stanley home. I say, "Let's go, Rangers!" What do you want from me? I have been a Blueshirt fan since I was seven. Too bad we can't bring back Louie Fontinato and Andy Bathgate to the lineup.

2

The New York Rangers ignited the trio of childhood pals Joey, Bob, and Lou, as well as the Madison Square Garden faithful, like a match in a haystack after the Blueshirts defeated the favored Islanders four games to two. Alas, the euphoria was short-lived. The team considered as the Yankees of hockey, the Montreal Canadians, ended the Ranger ride for the cup. After winning game 1 at the Montreal Forum and taking a lead in game 2, the Rangers succumbed to their "original six" rival, losing that second contest and the subsequent three games in a row.

"Those fuckin' Canadians are unbelievable."

"Guy Lafleur can kiss my hairy white ass."

"We had a good run."

The respective comments of Bob, Lou, and Joey were duly noted.

Eventually, May 1979 became the root for Robert Murphy month as the head baseball coach at Monsignor McClancy High School led his team to the Catholic High School Athletic Association (CHSAA) Class AA championship finals. His Crusaders would face the ever-present Stanners of Archbishop Molloy in a two out of three format for the title. "Somehow it doesn't seem fair," said his mom. "How can a mere Monsignor defeat an Archbishop?"

Joey, Lou, and Bob were all alumni of McClancy. The three had each starred on the baseball team, garnering second team all-city honors in their senior year, 1962. Joey was secretly thinking of doing a Sports

Chat article on the McClancy team and awaited the approval of the *Daily News* sports director. When the three-game playoff reached a deciding game, each team winning once, he got his wish. The ultimatum of his boss was simple: "Make it good, Kowalski. I wanna see the spirit of high school baseball in New York City come to life."

Game 3 was played at the home field of Molloy. The high school was located in the northwest section of Jamaica, Queens, an area commonly referred to as Briarwood. The attendees at the game included Joey and Susan, Lou and Grace, and of course, Bob's soon-to-be better half, Janet.

Lou was in prime "Crusader fan" mode for the contest. "Screw the Stanners, it's our time."

Joey had done some research before the deciding game. He wanted to add a little history to his column. He had no recollection of the origin of the Molloy nickname and knew it was incumbent to identify noted alumni and discuss the exploits of their renowned coach.

First, the nickname. Originally, the school was St. Ann's Academy, and the students were called St. Ann-ers, and thus evolved the one-word epithet the Stanners.

He also brushed up on the unsurpassed history of the school relative to New York City sports, particularly in basketball and baseball, where the Molloy status was at the summit. His recounting also identified several notable graduates, which included the following:

- Lou Carnesecca (1943) – who coached the basketball team before being replaced by the current coach, Jack Curran, in 1958 (We'll get to Curran again in due time.)
- Peter Vecsey (1961) – noted sports columnist for the *New York Daily News* and *New York Post*
- Kevin Joyce (1969) – who captained the 1972 USA Olympic basketball team
- Brian Winters (1970) – an NBA all-star

- Vitas Gerulaitis (1971) – professional tennis champion

"I worked with Vecsey at the *Daily News* for years," noted Joey as he discussed the upcoming matchup between McClancy and Molloy with Lou and Bob. "He graduated a year before we did. That bastard always busted my balls when he found out that I went to McClancy. Those freakin' Stanners almost always had our number. I did throw a two-hitter against them in our senior year though."

Lou can't help but bring up Kevin Joyce. "Joyce was one of the guys defending the inbound pass to that shithead Alexander Belov in the gold medal game at the 1972 Olympics in Berlin. Doug Collins had stolen a pass, was fouled, and converted two free throws to put us up by a point with three seconds on the clock. Then the worst officiating of all time cost us the game. What a freakin' joke that was. The referees wound up giving the Russians three chances to inbound from under our basket, and Belov wound up converting a layup at the buzzer. We protested the 51–50 final score and never accepted our silver medals. Hey, Joey, how did we miss that story for the Dopey Bastid book? The officials and timekeepers really deserved to be castrated that day."

Joey shook his head in the affirmative. "I definitely should have."

Bob spoke with admiration about his opposing coach, Jack Curran, who, in addition to baseball, also guided the fortunes of Molloy on the hardwood.

"Can you believe that guy? He's won more Coach of the Year awards than the number of years I have been coaching. Shit, he still holds the national high school record for consecutive wins. I think it was something like sixty-nine in a row."

"Close, Bob. It was sixty-eight," added Joey.

But this was 1979 and the Crusaders were almost on a par with Molloy during the regular season, winning twenty-one of twenty-six games, while their Queens rival recorded twenty-three victories against only three defeats—one of the losses to McClancy.

As his friends sat in the stands for the concluding contest, Bob sat in the dugout, with his conundrum whether to give a Knute Rockne– or Vince Lombardi–type discourse. He decided on just using Bob Murphy vernacular.

"Listen, you guys, you're here because you deserve to be. This team is far and away the best I have had the privilege to coach. Just go out and have fun. You know what, screw that, go kick some Stanner ass!"

The early going was favorable, at least on the field. Tommy Shea, the Crusader star center fielder, tripled in two runs in the top of the first inning, and the score held at 2–0 entering the bottom of the fourth.

In the stands, the attractive mother of Tommy Shea, Michelle, sat directly behind the Bob Murphy contingent. Lou and Joey both realized who she was after listening to her raucous cheering following her son's jaunt to third base in the opening inning. Lou had commented in a whisper to Joey.

"That's the mom that Bob played hide-the-sausage with last fall."

Earlier in that school year, Bob, who doubled as a history teacher, had concluded that Tommy Shea had plagiarized his term paper. He had called in Tommy's mother, Michelle, an only parent, to discuss the consequences of his actions. The meeting led to a date and a one-night stand. Tommy was excused from punishment.

Bob, in a tearful exchange with his best friends at Budd's bar, had revealed all a few days afterward. Although he was not engaged to Janet at the time, he had begun to see her after she separated from her, in Bob's words, "dickhead husband."

Michelle tapped Grace on the shoulder. "Hi, I'm Michelle Shea, Tommy's mom. Are you guys all friends of the coach?" Grace smiled and began introductions, ending with "and this is Bob's fiancée, Janet.

Michelle Shea responded to the future Mrs. Murphy. "You have one good-looking and sexy guy there, Janet. Treat him well."

Lou, knowing of Bob's brief tryst with Michelle, immediately tried to joke around. "C'mon, Michelle, you can't be serious about Bob being sexy."

Joey also endeavored to make light of the situation. "Are you sure you have the right guy, Michelle?"

Unfortunately, that line left an opening for a response from the attractive mother of the McClancy star center fielder. "Let's just say, I wouldn't kick him out of bed if he weren't engaged."

Janet got up and walked away under the pretense of a ladies' room visit and was followed by Susan and Grace. She sensed there was more to Michelle's comment than met the eye and had one terse statement for her friends. "I need to ask Bob about her."

Lou realized that Janet had her antenna up and quietly noted to Joey, "We have to let Murphy know what occurred here."

The 3–1 McClancy victory over Molloy was cause for rejoicing. Yet Janet was unusually quiet and pensive at the team celebration following her beau's championship triumph.

Author's note: the 1979 events pertaining to the Molloy– McClancy high school baseball season are fictitious.

Bob had been updated by his amigos. That evening he expected questions from his childhood girlfriend, who was now to become his wife. He decided not to wait. "Listen, hon, I have something to tell you."

Janet was initially quite perturbed but eventually took the high road with Bob. "Listen, Murphy, let's call it even. I couldn't wait for you and married that asshole, Richard. Then you played Don Juan with the mother of one of your students. I know it was before we got engaged, but it's very hurtful to me nonetheless. That's the end of ever causing pain in our relationship."

Janet actually had a clandestine occurrence that remained untold. She often questioned herself relative to whether she should tell her husband-to-be about her one- time sexual encounter with Lou even though it was on the evening of Grace's wedding to Tony Roma (later annulled) and at a time when she was totally disenchanted with her marriage to Richard Mitchell. Additionally, Bob was with his bimbo date from Brooklyn, Cynthia, and Janet sought out her friend Lou, who attended the wedding of his childhood sweetheart, Grace, stag.

Janet and Lou had a pact. No mention of this occurrence to Bob or Grace, or Susan and Joey for that matter.

With the help of their friends, the Bob and Janet relationship survived the Murphy transgression. The weekend following Bob's disclosure to Janet, Joey sat with Susan and recollected his friends' rueful confession to him and Lou the previous fall.

"Bob was disconsolate when he told us about Michelle Shea."

Susan somewhat jokingly questioned Joey about his fidelity. Joey may not have been expected to answer but he did anyway.

"I have always been faithful to you, babe."

Lou's explanation of the Murphy tryst to Grace did not go as smoothly after confessing to his future spouse that he had advised Bob, "Make sure it is a one and done with Michelle, but don't tell Janet."

"You told Bob what? That must mean you have a few things that you are hiding from me."

In actuality, Lou did have two events that required a declaration of guilt although neither was an indiscretion that directly involved Grace. His Camille story was revealed, and he was eventually acquitted by the Grace Caruso high court regarding the time he had succumbed to the sexual advances of the wife of a Manhattan College classmate. His Janet episode, on the evening of Grace's wedding to Tony Roma, remained undisclosed.

Joey and Lou talked the next day.

"Lou, you confessed to Grace about the time you screwed the wife of your college classmate?"

Joey, certainly the most quixotic of the three friends, was impressed at the forthrightness of his Italian buddy.

"It just seemed an appropriate time to bring it up. Hey, you know that imprudence on my part ate me up for years. I betrayed a friend. I still haven't forgiven myself. Lou then felt the need to come clean regarding his brief tryst with Janet. However, he realized he needed to talk to Janet first."

3

The Spectacular Bid victory in the Preakness Stakes at Pimlico preceded the Monsignor McClancy championship. Now, the Belmont Stakes stood between the magnificent stallion, whose heritage could be tracked to his famous grandsire, Bold Ruler, from being a third consecutive winner of the prestigious Triple Crown.

The Preakness, second of the three most important races for three-year-olds, had the horse racing experts comparing the marvelous thoroughbred with praise usually reserved for the great ones. Maybe, despite being bumped early, the 5½-length margin over the field in a record time of 1:54.2 was fodder for all the commotion. *Note: although the winning time of Secretariat in 1973 was deemed to be miscalculated.*

On June 9, Spectacular Bid left the starting gate at Belmont Park as the 1–5 choice of the bettors. This is despite rumors of a safety pin having penetrated his hoof and consideration given to his being scratched.

The early fractions—with Spectacular Bid close to the lead under the guidance (or as many astute horse racing buffs have pointed out—misguidance) of his teenage jockey, Ronnie Franklin—were ridiculously fast for the mile-and-a-half encounter, and Bid took the lead before three-fourths of a mile was completed.

Joey Kowalski, Bob Murphy, and Lou Marciano, who watched the race at Joey's condo, were not nearly as savvy in the world of saddles and bridles as they were in the major team sports. Yet all three were cognizant that the speedy early fractions could spell disaster over a mile and a half—a distance that would equate to an additional two furlongs (a quarter of a mile) farther than any of the three-year-old colts had ever experienced.

Bob proclaimed, "What the fuck is that kid doing?"

Lou rebutted with "Pull him back, you young little dickhead."

Joey had simply noted, "It's your race to lose, Ronnie, just ease up a little."

When the tiring Spectacular Bid was passed down the stretch by the 4–1 second choice, Coastal and had to settle for a third-place finish, the Monday morning quarterbacks were abundant. The focus was on questioning the trainer, Bud Delp, for allowing the colt to run after the apparent injury to the hoof and even more directly on the inferior ride of Franklin. The jockey admitted afterward that he had ridden a poorly judged race and that his lack of experience in riding the "ponies" over long distances may have cost his horse a chance of joining the select group of Triple Crown winners.

Several commentators even speculated that the trainer and jockey had been intent on imitating the unbelievable performance of Secretariat in 1973 by using tactics which sought to maximize the margin of victory.

Joe Kowalski's column on June 10 opined, "Ronnie Franklin and Bud Delp instigated the witnessing of a truly Unspectacular Bid."

CHAPTER IV

OH CAPTAIN, MY CAPTAIN

1

Baseball adorned the *Daily News* back page headlines in July and August, save for the day after the NBA draft. The broad smile of Magic Johnson, the first overall pick, was the sole interruption.

Here is the beginning of Joey Kowalski's Sports Chat article the day afterward.

Sports Chat by Joe Kowalski
June 26, 1979

Well, I guess the Knicks did OK yesterday. After the expected "hardship" selection of sophomore Magic Johnson by the Lakers, who had obtained the pick in a trade with the New Orleans Jazz, and with the Chicago Bulls opting for forward David Greenwood of UCLA, the Knicks went big. Bill Cartwright, the 7'1" center out of San Francisco University, was their choice.

The second team all-American averaged 24.5 points and 15.7 rebounds in his senior year.

Too bad the Knicks didn't have the foresight of the Celtics, though. Last year we took Michael Ray Richardson with the fourth overall pick, while the wisdom of Red Auerbach opted to gamble and select some unknown with the sixth pick. Yeah, a junior forward who was eligible for selection because he had sat out a year after originally enrolling at Indiana University. The risk for the Celtics was their requirement to sign him prior to this year's draft. Unfortunately for the Knicks, they did.

Larry Bird, who won just about every award imaginable this year, save for Magic taking home the trophy for NCAA tournament MVP, signed in time and will now take his skills to the land of Bill Russell, Bob Cousy, John Havlicek, Dave Cowens, and . . . this just gets too painful; I have to stop.

Lou Marciano relaxed at the home of his older brother, John, that evening. They discuss the NBA draft.

"Red Auerbach has to be the greatest mind in basketball," offered his brother.

"I always wanted to take that cigar he would light up on the bench after a victory was in hand and shove it up his ass. But you know what? I wish that bald-headed, pudgy little runt was guiding the Knicks!"

It rarely took Lou long to get to the point.

2

After the games played on Wednesday, August 1, the Yankees and Mets were both in trouble, each fourteen games out of first place in their respective eastern divisions.

The Yankees, in pursuit of their third consecutive championship, were a very respectable 58–48. The problem was that the Baltimore Orioles had won an astounding 72 games to easily lead the division. To make matters worse, the Pinstripes also stood behind their archrivals, the Red Sox, who were a solid 63 and 40, and the Milwaukee Brewers, who were two games behind Boston, in third place.

Needless to say, while George Steinbrenner retained lead partner control of the club, there was never a dull moment in the Bronx. The impulsive owner, who had made a midseason change the year before, replacing Billy Martin with Bob Lemon, decided to play "switchies." After a 34–31 start, it was Billy's back at the House That Ruth Built.

Meanwhile in the Borough of Queens, the Shea Stadium crowds struggled to exceed ten thousand as the last- place Mets still had their fans wondering why in hell they had traded Tom Seaver.

Bob, his rooting interests still with the Giants on the West Coast, was blunt. "They should get rid of Joe Torre and just hire Cheryl Tiegs to walk around the stadium in her bathing suit."

"I like that line, Bob, maybe I'll get it into one of my columns," exclaimed Joey.

"You can come up with something better than that, Kowalksi," added Lou behind a mischievous grin.

"Kiss my ass, Marciano, you wish you had thought of it" was Bob's rebuttal.

"Ease up, Murphy, you should be able to tell when I am busting your cookies by now. By the way, I have a trivia question for you two. Who was the guy that the Mets picked up from Cleveland in 1962 for a player to be named later, who eventually was returned to the Indians as the player to be named later? In effect he was traded for himself!"

"Got you this time, Marciano," Joey says proudly. "It was Harry Chiti."

3

August 2, 1979, was an off day for the Yankees.

Joey Kowalski was sitting at his *New York Daily News* desk, pondering about the subject matter for an upcoming column, when he heard a disconcerting report. There was a tragedy in the baseball world and it involved the Yankees. Thurman Munson, their all-star catcher and captain, had died in a plane crash.

Soon, CBS, NBC, and ABC were covering the incident. Munson, who had been taking flying lessons for several years, died while practicing landings at the Akron-Canton Regional Airport. His Cessna Citation jet had clipped a tree, fallen short of the runway, and burst into flames. Two passengers onboard, the flight instructor and a friend of Thurman's, survived.

Love of family was the principal reason that Munson wanted to fly. Frequently homesick, he sought a way to be with his wife and children more often. His third touch- and-go practice landing on the second of August 1979 made that a moot point.

Lou's secretary, whom he affectionately called Cha Cha, knocked gently on his town of Babylon director of engineering and traffic safety office door. "Lou, I know that you are busy but I thought that you would want to know . . ."

The die-hard Yankee fan was devastated. Tears soon trickled down his cheek.

After returning home early that evening, Lou called Joey and inquired as to whether he would be writing about Munson in his next-day column. When Joey indicated that he wanted to digest the situation and save his Sports Chat tribute until the weekend, Lou was pleased.

"Listen, buddy, I have a few thoughts that I'd like to share with you. Maybe you can integrate them into your column on Munson. How about meeting at Budd's in a half hour? I'll see if Bob can get down there also."

Joey got much more information from Lou than he could ever have imagined and graciously thanked him for the insights elicited.

Bob was surprisingly sentimental as he absorbed the Lou Marciano narrative. He also brought up Roberto Clemente's untimely death in a 1972 plane crash while in the role of a Good Samaritan seeking to provide provisions to assist the victims of the earthquake in Managua, Nicaragua. The three even discussed two other plane crash tragedies: Rocky Marciano's death in 1969 and the night the music died—the tragic 1959 accident that saw rock n roll legends Buddy Holly, Ritchie Valens, and J. P. Richardson, the Big Bopper, perish.

The next day, on Friday, August 3, the Yankees paid tribute to Munson at the stadium. The pregame ceremony with the first-place Orioles saw the starters standing at their defensive positions. The home plate area, the domicile of Thurman Munson since his Rookie of the Year award- winning season of 1970, was left unoccupied. Not until after

- a prayer by Cardinal Terrence Cooke,
- a moment of silence with scoreboard pictorials of Munson,
- Robert Merrill singing "America the Beautiful," and
- an eight-minute standing ovation from over fifty- one thousand

did the starting Yankee catcher for the game, Jerry Narron, come out of the dugout.

Joey's Sports Chat tribute to Thurman Munson appeared in that Sunday's *New York Daily News*.

Sports Chat by Joe Kowalski

August 5, 1979

I was privileged to vote for the Hall of Fame this year—my first chance to recognize the greats of America's pastime. While I realized the importance of that endeavor, I consider it much more of an honor to discuss Thurman Munson with you today.

First of all, I'd like to offer my sincere condolences to his wife, Diana, and his three children, Tracy, Kelly, and Michael. I am somewhat at a loss for words, certainly regarding Thurman's four-year-old son.

What I wanted to relate to you folks today was a conversation I had with my two best friends. I have mentioned both of these guys often because they each know more about sports than I do. Well, at least as much, anyway.

After the three of us discussed Thurman's accomplishments—

- Rookie of the Year in 1970
- seven-time all-star
- 1976 MVP
- heart and soul of the Yankees and role in the 1976 AL Pennant and 1977 and 1978 World Series championships
- first captain in Yankee history since Lou Gehrig
- extending the Yankee catching legacy from Bill Dickey, Yogi Berra, and Elston Howard.

—and then recounted his strained relationship with Reggie and feud with Carlton Fisk, my friend Lou brought up a story from our high school days. He reminisced about an assignment on Abraham Lincoln. I had barely recollected our obligation to research our sixteenth president.

In any event, he evoked having chosen to write about Lincoln's untimely death. You know the details, so I won't get into them here. In his review he became enamored by a Walt Whitman poem written shortly after the President's demise, "Oh Captain, My Captain."

On his way home from work last Thursday, he thought about Munson and the crash of his Cessna Citation jet at the Akron-Canton Airport. He couldn't pinpoint why, but Lincoln and the poem became vivid in his contemplation. He just couldn't get either out of his mind.

He began to feel a connection between Thurman and Abe. "There intertwined as captains who died tragically," he added. Then he became sentimental, making reference to comments from Thurman's two best friends on the Yankees, Bobby Murcer and Lou Piniella. "I then started thinking that it could just as easily have been two of us talking about the third," he said.

After we ordered a round of beers, Lou handed me a copy of the Walt Whitman poem and I read it. Then my other friend, Bob, did the same. "One more thing," offered Lou, "Munson was learning how to fly because he wanted to be able to spend more time with his family."

So I write this column thinking of what it would be like to lose a best friend, or for my wife, Susan, and my daughter, Grace Janet, to be without their husband and father. Regarding the former, I pray to God that I have my friends with me for a long time. Relative to the latter I hope that my accomplishments would come close to measuring up to the captains Abe Lincoln and Thurman Munson.

The final verse of "Oh Captain, My Captain" by Walt Whitman:

My Captain does not answer, his lips are pale and still; My father does not feel my arm, he has no pulse nor will;

The ship is anchor'd safe and sound, its voyage closed and done;

From fearful trip, the victor ship, comes in with object won

"Exult, O shores, and ring O bells!

But I, with mournful tread,

Walk the deck my captain lies,

Fallen cold and dead".

On August 6, the entire Yankee team attended the funeral of their thirty-two-year-old captain in Canton, Ohio. Eulogies by Bobby Murcer and Lou Piniella left most without a dry eye. Then the team flew back to New York for the nationally televised ABC *Monday Night Baseball* encounter against the first-place Orioles at Yankee Stadium.

Trailing 4–0, the Yankees rallied on a three-run home run in the seventh and a two-run single in the bottom of the ninth for the 5–4 win. All five runs were driven in by Thurman's good friend Bobby Murcer.

The image of Thurman Munson is displayed on the Yankee Stadium big screen scoreboard the day after he was tragically killed in a plane crash on August 2, 1979. Third baseman, Graig Nettles, has his head bowed. The value of Munson to the New York Yankees of the 1970s went far beyond what could be measured statistically. Thurman was the team captain, the first to hold that honor since Lou Gehrig. He was a stalwart behind the plate in the lineage of Bill Dickey, Yogi Berra, and Elston Howard. Munson was the 1970 AL Rookie of the Year, the 1976 AL MVP, a seven-time all-star and hit over .300 five times. He was at his best when it counted the most, hitting .373 in three World Series appearances.

CHAPTER V

DUAL WEDDING

1

Janet Poska and Robert Murphy
and
Grace Caruso and Lou Marciano

Cordially invite you to attend their

On the tenth day of November 1979
Ceremonial Mass: St. Joan of Arc Church, 4:30 p.m.
Reception: Villa Russo, 6:30 p.m.
RSVP - REGRETS ONLY by Oct. 5

The above invitation was mailed to 294 guests on August 31, 1979.

2

"No way, Lou, we split everything. I don't want to hear any more about it."

Bob Murphy was adamant. It didn't matter to him that the respondents to the dual wedding would be disproportionate and favor the Caruso-Marciano duo. This was principally due to the rife number of family members that Lou Marciano expected.

"C'mon, Murphy, that's not fair to you and Janet. It's easy enough to pay for this by the number of guests we each have."

"Forget about it. There's the band and the flowers and all that shit, we split it even and that's it." Bob had the concurrence of Janet on the issue.

Lou finally gave in. Secretly he told Grace that at the time of the wedding he would see what the difference was and "make it up to Janet and Bob somehow" down the road. Then the lightbulb went off.

"Screw Murphy. You know what, we are going to pay for the entire honeymoon cruise, us and them. I'll make those arrangements with my buddy from the Royal Caribbean."

Grace concurred. "That will be a nice surprise for them, Lou. Are you sure that we all agreed on the cruise destination?"

"You confirm that with Janet. We were talking about the eight-day excursion out of the city with stops in Curacao, St. Thomas, St. Marten, and Aruba. I am not sure of the order of the layovers, but those are the four islands."

Grace followed up with Janet and validated Lou's identification. Now there was only one potential snag. Susan and Joey began to insinuate that they would like to come along.

"Can you imagine if we went with you guys? That would be unbelievable." Susan Kowalski sought a reaction from Grace and to her glee got a "If you two came along, it would be the best!"

Grace gave Lou the heads-up and his reaction was typical. "No problem, I'll call and advise Barry to give us a third room. I'll get a break for them too, I'm sure."

And so it would be, the core six in the Caribbean together. Friends for life.

3

There was one Joey Kowalski Sports Chat column that was a significant diversion from the customary major sport coverage of the *Daily News* journalistic maven.

"I just have to write about the US Tennis Open final because of the guys playing in it. It is New York squared." And so it was. Joey had defended his choice of topics to Bob and Lou. They begrudgingly coalesced to his decision.

Sports Chat by Joe Kowalski
September 10, 1979

"If I can make it there, I'll make it anywhere." Liza Minnelli gave us a great rendition of "New York, New York" in the film, and I understand that Frank Sinatra is recording the song for his next album. Although he won't be in a singing competition with Liza or Frank, John McEnroe, with his convincing straight-set victory yesterday over his friend Vitas Gerulaitis in the US Open Tennis final, assuredly is crooning the melody in the shower and believing that he has arrived.

First of all, I ain't no tennis buff. I am a New Yorker though, and I was proud to see two local products in the finals of our country's preeminent tennis event.

Vitas Gerulaitis was born in Brooklyn, a graduate of Archbishop Molloy HS in Queens, and a one-year attendee of Columbia University, my alma mater. Charismatic both on and off the court, the tennis aficionados I have spoken to, all have marveled at the quickness of his hands at the net and his dazzling court coverage.

The Gerulaitis proficiency in the game, where "love" is used more often in one match than I have used in my whole life (sorry, honey), was no match for the brat-like kid from Douglaston, Queens.

Born in Wiesbaden, Germany, McEnroe first plied his craft at the Douglaston Tennis Club as an eight-year-old, then at the Eastern Lawn Tennis Association, and soon he was a stalwart at the Port Washington Tennis Academy.

As an eighteen-year-old amateur in 1977, John teamed with his childhood friend from Queens, Mary Carillo, to win the mixed doubles title at the French Open and then gave Jimmy Connors a run for his money before succumbing in four sets in the semifinals at Wimbledon.

After enrolling at Stanford, he won the NCAA singles title in 1978 and, before joining the pro tour later that year, also led his school to the team championship. His success as a professional was expeditious as he garnered victory in five tournaments, including a Masters Grand Prix victory over Arthur Ashe. (I really like that guy, by the way).

John McEnroe is now twenty and is the US Open champion. Pancho Gonzalez, I guy I did root for as a young teen, was slightly younger than John when he claimed victory in the Queens event in 1948.

Earlier in the Open tournament, McEnroe won the doubles title with Peter Fleming. Now, after disposing of Vitas, he has his first major singles title. It would appear that John is on the precipice of many more if he can control his penchant for upsetting umpires. I understand one guy recently uttered, "I wish that André the Giant would place him in a bear hug and have him whining like a four-year-old whose ice cream cone has just fallen to the ground."

Good luck, John. "If you can make it here . . ."

"Not bad Kowalski, it actually sounded like you knew what the hell you were talking about." Robert Murphy had enjoyed the article.

4

Susan Kowalski, with her mother and mother-in-law alternating in watching Grace Janet, was able to resume her English teaching position in the New York City school system. Her challenge for the semester was an advanced college-credit course regarding twentieth- century American poets. Her approbation for a student who, in an initial report submission, had identified his favorite American poets as Bob Dylan and Paul Simon was likewise venerated by her husband and favorite two couples, Janet and Bob and Grace and Lou. Lou was particularly in awe of the "outside of the box" thinking of the high school senior.

"I always felt that those two guys were special talents, even more for their songwriting than their singing. I especially like "Positively Fourth Street" and "Bridge over Troubled Water." Lou cannot resist an excerpt recital of each.

> *I wish that for just one time you could stand inside my*
> *shoes, And just for that one moment, I could be you.*
> *Yes, I wish that for just one time, you could stand*
> *inside my shoes,*
> *You'd know what a drag it is to see you.*
>
> *If you need a friend,*
> *I'm sailing right behind.*
> *Like a bridge over troubled water,*
> *I will ease your mind.*

Not to be outdone by her husband, Grace was up to the task of identifying a woman whose prowess as a song writer preceded her notoriety as a vocalist, Carole King.

The soon to be Grace Marciano noted that although the poetic lyrics of "You've Got a Friend" were closely attributed to Carole's good friend, James Taylor, that she in fact had originally recorded her own song.

Susan was appreciative of the insight of Grace which afforded recognition to a female artist.

5

With the dual wedding day approaching, the two brides- to-be, meticulously prepared every aspect of their wedding ceremony and reception. The guys took a "let them do whatever they want" attitude except for a few elements.

Bob picked the band, finally settling on a six-piece group, the Dirty Half Dozen, a highly acclaimed ensemble from Bay Ridge, Brooklyn. They had the diversity to play the current hits and still cater to the older family members with Irish, Polish, and Italian songs. There was also a clandestine reason for the Murphy selection.

"That lead singer, Kim, is a real hot number. All the guys will be dancing with their tongues hanging out."

Lou knew he had to carefully review the menu. In the Marciano family, good food came first. He also realized that the menu would need to include some Polish and Irish fare and insisted that the cocktail hour include kielbasa and shepherd's pie, in addition to the hot and cold, principally Italian-style buffet. Salad and lasagna would precede the main course choices consisting of veal sorrentino, chicken parmesan, prime rib, or stuffed fillet of sole.

"Both of our families love Italian food too, Lou." Bob spoke for his Polish bride, Janet, and for his own Irish contingent.

Bob and Lou were invigorated as they carefully reviewed the liquor to be provided and discussed the choices with the Villa Russo manager.

"Only top-shelf liquors and make sure you have Jameson's for shots and Irish coffee later on."

"For the dessert table we'll need to have sambuca or your best anisette to go with the espresso for anyone who wants it. Oh yeah, make the scotch Dewar's and also have a twelve-year scotch available, either Johnnie Walker Black or Chivas Regal."

Murphy had spoken initially; Marciano added the additional alcoholic beverage requests.

The most difficult decision of the two couples was the selection of wedding songs. Their taste in music was analogous. Often Janet and Grace would both proclaim, "I love that song too," and Bob and Lou would just shake their heads in realization that the final choices for their opening dance of the evening could require compromise. Finally, with the assistance of Susan, each bride-to-be was satisfied.

"You Are So Beautiful" by Joe Cocker and "Just the Way You Are" by Billy Joel would guide the initial dance steps of Janet and Bob and Grace and Lou respectively.

Joey offered one piece of advice. "Remember, guys, no putting your hands on their asses for the first dance."

6

The dual wedding mass at St. Joan of Arc Church had several nuances. Father Mike, the favorite priest of the core six while growing up in Jackson Heights, Queens, was the choice to perform the ceremony. He gladly accepted the invite despite his fifty-mile-plus drive from St. Margret of Scotland Parish in Selden, Long Island, where he now served as pastor. He was even gracious enough to pick up Sister Marie Angela on the way. The eighth-grade teacher of the group at the school bearing the same name as the church now served in an administrative position at the diocesan offices in Rockville Center, Nassau County.

"Ave Maria" was sung by Grace's first cousin Jessica, a rendition which was so poignant that few desiccated eyes could subsequently be found. Of course, with Lou as one of the wedding participants, there had to be a touch a humor. During his vows, amid laughter from most, he held his fingers crossed behind his back.

His mother saw no humor in his action and afterward vehemently admonished her son. "Louis [his mother always used his full name when he was in trouble], don't you know it's a sin to be disrespectful in church. You had better ask God to forgive you."

At 6:30 p.m., the festivities began at Villa Russo. The cocktail "hour and a half" was preplanned to afford ample time for all attendees to partake in the wide assortment of ethnic delights, albeit with Italian dominance.

Soon thereafter, the Villa Russo emcee was heard introducing the wedding party, a total of six bridesmaid- groomsmen couples. The maid of honor, Susan Kowalski, held the top female role for both Janet and Grace, with her two escorts (husband, Joey, the best man for Bob, and Lou's best man, his brother, John).

Grace and Lou were the first of the newlywed couples to be introduced. A thunderous applause was heard after "and for the first time as husband and wife, Mr. and Mrs. Lou Marciano."

You might have thought that Bob and Janet would have received similar adulation once their names were presented to the Villa Russo throng. Well, they would have, except for the laughter that equaled the emotional tribute. Lou Marciano had done it again. A twenty-dollar tip to the emcee was all it took for him to modify the name introduction from Mr. and Mrs. Robert Murphy to Mr. and Mrs. Robert Poska, using Janet's maiden name.

"He'll be whipped for the rest of his life anyway, so he might as well take her name now."

Joey Kowalski convulsed after hearing the name change and again upon hearing Lou's follow-up comment.

There were three wedding toasts: the maid of honor, Susan Kowalski, for both Janet and Grace; Joey Kowalski, the best man for Bob Murphy; and John Marciano, the best man for his brother, Lou. The latter, having a surprise for his new sister-in-law and brother, had asked if he could say his few words about his brother, prior to the couple's first dance.

John, having already polished off four Johnnie Walker Black's on the rocks was in good form.

"My brother, Lou, has unfortunately always taken a backseat to me. Actually, as he was growing up, he took more than that since I often had to keep his butt in line. I can still kick his you-know-what."

"Bring it on, big brother." Lou couldn't resist the interruption.

John continued his discourse, reminiscent of one of the comics at a Dean Martin and friends roast.

"Lou was always second best in the Marciano brothers' pecking order, and I am not just referring to age. My younger brother was also number two in looks, the runner-up in intelligence, and never achieved entry to the winner circle regarding the appendage in his jockey shorts. OK, maybe I lied. He has always been number one relative to the size of his schnoz."

Bob and Joey were thoroughly enjoying the ribbing targeted at Lou by his older sibling. They each interject for all to hear.

"Give it to him, John."

"No holds barred, big brother Marciano."

John, acknowledged his brothers' two best friends with a smile and a thumbs up.

"Well, I guess I can praise my younger brother for his diligence in staying in shape and looking good in his tux for this occasion. He lost ten pounds. The last pound came yesterday. He cut his nose hairs."

Grace, who was trying her best not to laugh at her spouse's expense, lost it. After gaining her composure she loudly proclaimed, "C'mon John, it was only a half of a pound."

John had the full attention of his audience as his demeanor became momentarily serious.

"OK, before my mom comes up here and gives me a beating for belittling her precious baby boy, I would be remiss if I didn't say a few words about Lou's choice of a forever mate." He then looked toward the newest Mrs. Marciano in the family. "Grace is beautiful and intelligent and has a heart as big as they come. I am ecstatic to have her as a sister-in-law. In fact, I never had a sister . . . now I do."

John needed a few seconds to regain his composure. He then revealed the reason for his request to speak before either Susan or Joey.

"Grace and Lou have chosen to dance to the song 'Just the Way You Are' by Billy Joel. I just happen to know Billy, so I asked him to do me a favor. Joining the band to sing one of his biggest hits is my friend and a great songwriter, musician, and vocalist . . . Mr. Piano Man, Billy Joel."

The boisterous applause of the just under three hundred attendees was interrupted as Grace momentarily left her husband to plant a big hug and kiss on John, and then run to the microphone to do likewise to Billy.

To the delight of Janet and Bob, John had also arranged for Billy to sing "You Are So Beautiful," the tender Joe Cocker ballad.

John Marciano's Billy Joel surprise made him number one with each of the two wedding couples. Well, that may have been slightly redundant. He already was number one with Lou.

After the second wedding song, Susan Kowalski arose and took the microphone from Billy. "Show-off," she proclaimed with a beaming smile.

"I have heard of tough acts to follow but this is ridiculous. John's commentary was difficult enough, then Billy Joel, you have got to be kidding me."

Susan didn't disappoint the wedding guests with her genuine observations on behalf of the two best friends she thought of as sisters. Janet and Grace were not the only two sobbing when she completed her dialogue.

Joey Kowalski hugged and kissed his wife and then took the mike. He was the best man for Bob Murphy but knew a few words about Lou Marciano, his other best friend, was in order. Before his Murphy roast, Joey was sentimental in his recollection of Lou having been near death as a thirteen-year-old and how happy he was to be with him on his wedding day.

"OK, everybody, enough of the mushie stuff. Time to turn your attention to the slick Irishman sitting to my right."

The next five minutes had the family and friends of Robert Murphy and the whole damn crowd for that matter in stitches. It was obvious that the noted sportswriter, not ordinarily one to be the potentate of humor, had prepared for the occasion well—his recollection of several events as eighth graders at St. Joan of Arc and as students at McClancy High School was especially hilarious.

"Hey, Lou, am I allowed to tell about the time that Murphy tried to fart in our freshman year biology class and soiled himself?"

"No, Joey, let's keep that as a secret among the three of us."

Joey's most highly applauded tale was fabricated—a fictional reminiscence regarding one of Bob's dates before he reconnected with Janet.

"I was talking to his date and explaining to her that, after you die, you get reincarnated, but have to come back as a different creature. 'Oh really?' she said. 'Then I want to come back as a cow.' I looked at her incredulously and replied, 'You obviously haven't been paying attention.'"

Bob arose upon the completion of the Kowalski diatribe. He pointed at his good friend and, amid the type of joviality often witnessed in their youth, uttered, "Kowalski, your sports column sucks. Screw you and the horse you rode in on. And by the way, Duke could never even shine Willie's shoes."

"You tell him, Murphy, hit him with a kielbasa breath joke."

The Lou Marciano comment preceded another dual wedding highlight as Billy Joel drew the loudest ovation of the evening with his rendition of "Piano Man." The majority of the wedding guests joined in during the chorus

> Sing us a song, you're the piano man
>
> Sing us a song tonight
>
> Well we're all in the mood for a melody
>
> And you've got us feelin' alright

The wedding couples switched partners during the band's rendition of "Yesterday." Lou took the opportunity to question Janet.

"I think we have to tell Bob and Grace what happened between us on the night of Grace's wedding to that gumba, Tony Roma. I know it was over five years ago now, but it has been on my mind."

"Not tonight, Lou. I don't want anything to spoil this evening. Neither of them was directly affected at the time anyway. I was married but very unhappy with Richard, and Bob was with a date that night. You had gone stag and consoled me when you saw me crying in the flower gardens outside the reception hall. It was my fault. I came on to you."

"Just think about it, Janet."

7

The Caribbean cruise honeymoon of Janet and Robert Murphy and Grace and Louis Marciano was nothing short of spectacular. The late addition to the excursion of Susan and Joseph Kowalski had the three couples wondering if any earthly sovereign ever experienced a more memorable expedition.

Several highlights include the following:

- The term coined by Joey was *double breakfast*—a description of his two friends and himself in what became a daily morning ritual. First, there was breakfast with the girls on the ninth floor, then "walking it off"—an excruciating two-flights-of- stairs trip for the buffet breakfast served on the eleventh level of the ship.
- In Curacao, as the girls shopped for jewelry, the guys barhopped and drank with the locals. They barely made it back to the ship on time and then procrastinated further as they approached the ramp to the Royal Caribbean. The three chose to see who would have a photo taken with a boa constrictor draped around his neck. Bob, the close victor in the "most inebriated" contest, also prevailed in the "three-person choose," which dated back to their 1950s childhood. The photo of Bob, with the snake seemingly ready to strangle the happily smiling Irishman, was a classic.
- Grace and Lou won the "hustle contest" over a field of over fifty couples. Janet and Bob finished third and were claiming foul regarding Grace's winking at one of the male judges.

- Susan was the lead Supreme as she and her two friends, delighted the ship's audience in their karaoke rendition of "Stop! In the Name of Love."
- The two Polacks, Janet Poska Murphy and Joey Kowalski, changed partners to team up to a Polka, which drew rave applause from the ship's captain and garnered an invitation to the six for dinner at the captain's table the following evening.
- Lou finished second in the blackjack tournament. He appeared to be headed for first place until the last hand of the event. The dealer, with 15, drew a 6, and bested a pissed-off Marciano, who had held with 20. "He pulled that card out of his ass."
- The bartender at one Aruba hotspot had the core six in stitches with "the cost of living has now gotten so bad that my wife is having sex with me again. She can't afford the batteries."
- A new acquaintance met on the ship may have had the best story of all, albeit told in jest. "My wife asked me which of her girlfriends I would want her to ask for a threesome on my birthday. I replied, "Bambi and Crystal." Who knew I was only supposed to give her one name."
- Susan O'Connor Kowalski, with the concurrence of her husband, Joey, bought special rings for everyone at a ship display table. "It's the least we could do, Joey, in appreciation for being invited on their honeymoons." The Irish claddagh rings, arguably one of the most culturally rich pieces of jewelry ever recorded in history, were a huge success with Janet, Bob, Grace, and Lou. Their appreciation was boundless. The ring displays hands holding a heart, and denotes friendship and togetherness.

The last evening in his cabin, with the ship expected to reach New York City the following day, Lou was introspective as he lay in bed. Grace was sleeping with her head comfortably resting on his chest. He was now a married man, and he felt assured that his choice of a mate would last an eternity. *Who has it better than me?* he thought to himself. *A loving family, best of friends, and now I have the beautiful gal who I always wanted beside me, as my wife.*

He was now getting horny but decided not to awake Grace. He knew he needed a distraction. "What were the Mick's Triple Crown numbers in 1956? Oh yeah, 353 BA, 52 homers, and 130 RBIs."

The photo above depicts a claddagh ring. Made in Ireland, the ring denotes friendship and togetherness.

CHAPTER VI

DO YOU BELIEVE IN MIRACLES?

1

It was official; Joe Kowalski would cover the 1980 Winter Olympics for the *New York Daily News*, specifically the US ice hockey squad. His patriotism was putatively beyond reproach, yet his feelings were mixed. He was not enamored by the fact that he would be away from his daughter, Grace Janet, his wife, Susan, and his good friends.

"Lake Placid, New York in the winter? I'm going to be freezing my nuts off."

Sports Chat by Joe Kowalski
February 10, 1980

This will be my last column before I devote my full attention to the US hockey squad. I leave for Lake Placid today. I just wanted to get something off of my chest before I departed.

I have waited a few weeks to congratulate my childhood idol Duke Snider on his election into the Hall of Fame. Damn, it took my fellow baseball writers eleven times to finally get it right. All of a sudden, Duke is worthy—a reflection of his having been included on almost 87 percent of the ballots. What the hell took so long? Now, maybe next year, my cohorts will see the light regarding Gil Hodges. I certainly hope so; he only has a few years of eligibility left. Oh yeah, congrats to Al Kaline too. The Detroit Tiger perennial all-star was a no-brainer in his first year of consideration for the Hall, at least to 340 of the 385 voters. It remains puzzling to me how the other forty-five writers could have the gall to deprive Kaline, a fantastic all-around ballplayer, from inclusion on their ballot even if it was his first year of eligibility. I have heard the refrain "He'll get in eventually anyway. He does not need my vote in the first year." What a crock. That kind of thinking kept Joe DiMaggio waiting until his third year. Disgraceful!

We have a job to do as sportswriters. Honesty, integrity, and the best use of the intelligence our Creator has given us should be paramount to those of us with the honor of selecting players for the hallowed placement of their plaque in Cooperstown. I understand that the voting is subjective based on the inexact guidelines for induction. Not everybody could see a clear picture this year for including a guy like Orlando Cepeda on their yes list like I did. That being said, all of you who over the years have omitted Willie Mays, Mickey Mantle, Stan Musial, Ted Williams, and the like on their first-year ballots should be ashamed. You are not deserving of a vote.

OK, time for me to get off my high horse, but I tell you what. If you agree with me, send me a note. Am I crazy?

Twenty years ago, the United States won Olympic gold in Squaw Valley, California. The second-to-the-last game was over a highly favored USSR squad 3–2. Jack McCartan, the US goaltender, was stellar. For us to get past the Soviet squad this year, Jim Craig, our Olympic netminder, will need to become a combination of Glenn Hall, Jaques Plante, and Terry Sawchuk. Damn, those guys were great when I was growing up.

Geez, I did say the 1960 Winter Games were in California, didn't I? And where am I going?

Bob Murphy was the first of Joey's two best friends to commend him on the article. "Way to go, Kowalski, you were right on. Some of those dopey bastards don't deserve to have a vote."

Lou Marciano had not read the Sports Chat column until early that evening. Since Joey was en route to Lake Placid, his admiration regarding the forthrightness of his friend was conveyed through a telephone conversation to Susan Kowalski.

"I just finished reading your husband's column, Susan. You should be proud of him, he's the best."

"Yeah, and he's cute too."

Susan laughed when Lou added, "Don't push it, Susan."

2

Sports Chat by Joe Kowalski
February 13, 1980

On the surface some may say that the 2–2 tie versus Sweden was a "kiss your sister" outcome. Not so in this case. The USA victory was dramatic; Bill Baker's goal, assisted by Mark Pavelich and Buzz Schneider, came with just twenty-seven seconds remaining in the contest, hopefully even a harbinger of better things to come. By the way, our first goal was scored by Dave Silk, the Boston University forward, who hopes that he will soon be skating professionally for the New York Rangers. Don't despair, Islander fans. You have an excellent defenseman coming your way—Ken Morrow, out of the University of Bowling Green.

More importantly, the international amateur hockey experts all felt that the US tie with one of the teams vying for a silver or bronze medal was a highly positive result for the red, white, and blue. Just in case you are not into the international hockey scene, the facile and near unanimous choice of the writers covering this event for the gold medal, regardless of what country they are from, is the USSR.

When I first learned that I would be covering hockey at these Olympic Games, I realized that politics could govern what is supposedly the ultimate of sporting event purity. The overriding question of whether the USSR—do you mind if I refer to them as the Russians?—would even participate in the Winter Olympics during a time when US-Soviet relations are so severely strained was dubious at best. Would the Russians come to Lake Placid? If so, and perhaps regardless of the Soviet decision, would the US, with the cold war created by the Soviet invasion of Afghanistan, travel to Moscow for the 1980 Summer Games? Certainly, President Carter, as well as the rest of our nation, also remains gravely concerned about the fifty-two hostages being detained in Iran for over three months. So much for the limpidness of the Olympics.

Well, the country that has won consecutive hockey gold medals every fourth year since the USA astonishing 1960 upset is here. The international hockey powerhouse, the USSR, who was 5–3–1 against NHL teams earlier this year, narrowly eschewed defeat their opening game. Yeah right; they just squeaked by Japan, 16–0.

Back to our boys. Let me start with the identification of the roster. From what I have heard, after going through the rigors of Head Coach Herb Brooks's grueling regimen, they deserve the adulation. Let's root for the guys that engender the enthusiasm of the chant "USA, USA, USA."

From the University of Minnesota, which is also where Herb Brooks plies his hockey trade:

Bill Baker (D), Neil Broten (F), Steve Christoff (F), Steve Janaszak (G), Rob McClanahan (F), Mike Ramsey (D), Buzz Schneider (F), Eric Strobel (F), Phil Verchota (F)

From Boston University:
Jim Craig (G), Mike Eruzione (F), Jack O'Callaghan (D), Dave Silk (F)

From the University of Minnesota Duluth:
John Harrington (F), Mark Pavelich (F)

From the University of Wisconsin:
Mark Johnson (F), Bob Suter (D)

From Bowling Green State University:
Ken Morrow (D), Mark Wells (F)

From the University of North Dakota:
Dave Christian (D)

I should also mention the assistant coach of the squad, Craig Patrick, whose family is so closely linked with National Hockey League history. Craig was a teammate of Herb Brooks on the 1967 US National Team.

Joey called Susan after writing the article. "Hey, babe, it's freakin' cold up here. I could use you to warm me up. How is my other best girl?"

"Grace Janet is great, but she misses you a lot. Say hello to her."

Joey's best baby talk had his daughter smiling angelically.

3

Bob Murphy, with prevalence toward graphic language, began his phone conversation response with "Screw you, Marciano." Unfortunately for him, the caller was not Lou Marciano, who was known for his practical jokes. Murphy mistakenly associated the caller with his Italian amigo.

At the other end of the invention most prominently associated with Alexander Graham Bell (except for the father of Lou Marciano, who insisted that the credit belonged to Innocenzo Manzetti—I wonder why) was Lou Carnesecca.

On the recommendation of Jack Curran, the esteemed baseball and basketball coach at Molloy High School, and behest of the St. John's athletic director, Carnesecca was asked to call Murphy to solicit him for the head coach position of the St. John's University varsity baseball team.

After a heartfelt apology to Little Louie, Murphy listened intently to the offer. He then called Lou Marciano.

"Marciano, you won't believe what just happened."

"What's that, Murphy? You found out that you can get it up again?"

"No, Lou, you really have to hear this."

A call to his wife, Janet, was followed by leaving a message for Joey. Bob agreed to a meeting with the athletic director and Carnesecca at 5:00 p.m. the following afternoon to more formally discuss the offer.

He was gratified by the proposition but began to question whether, as a graduate of each, he should even consider leaving McClancy High School for the Redmen of St. John's. At home that evening, Janet was clear with her spouse.

"Don't go nuts thinking about it until you have a chance to speak with them. It does seem like the opportunity of a lifetime though, especially if you get to continue teaching history at St. John's."

A return call from Joey Kowalski mimicked Janet's advice. Unbeknownst to Bob, Joey was cognizant of the soon- to-be vacant head baseball coach position and had recommended Bob to the athletic director, who in turn began his due diligence process on Murphy.

"I think you'd be a great fit there, Bob, and it is your alma mater. It certainly makes sense to listen."

4

After their opening tie with the Swedes, Joey Kowalski's columns appeared in the *New York Daily News* following each of the impressive USA team victories in the four blue division contests as follows:

- February 14: USA 7 – Czechoslovakia 3
- February 16: USA 5 – Norway 1
- February 18: USA 7 – Romania 2
- February 20: USA 4 – West Germany 2

Their 4–0–1 record catapulted the red, white, and blue into the medal round; enthusiasm around the United States was endemic. This was certainly quite an accomplishment considering that the USA was the overall seventh-ranked team entering the Games behind the USSR, Czechoslovakia, Sweden, Canada, Finland, and West Germany.

There was only one minor problem. Although the standings exhibited the USA and Sweden with identical entries, the Swedes were awarded first place on the basis of their one-goal scoring advantage. The second place USA troops would be required to face the first-place team in the red division. Who might that be? You got it—the Soviet Union.

Sports Chat by Joe Kowalski
February 21, 1980 (excerpt)

Our boys have defied the odds. The final four (no, not the NCAA basketball tournament, you bananas) is constituted by the USA, Sweden, Finland, and the indomitable force of the USSR. The latter merely outscored opponents by a margin of 40 goals (51–11), while posting a perfect 5–0 record.

Our boys are led by the goaltending of Jim Craig, whose 2.0 goals against average is second only to the Swedish Goalie, Pelle Lindberg, the scoring of Buzz Schneider (4G, 3A), Rob McClanahan (4G, 3A), and Mark Johnson (2G,5A), and from where I stand anyway, a well-conceived wide- open style, introduced to our college hockey stalwarts by Coach Herb Brooks. Puck movement is the mantra. A basketball analogy: the NY Knicks in the late sixties and early seventies, under Red Holzman, hit the open man.

Tomorrow will be the reckoning for our youthful squadron, with eighteen of our twenty players twenty-two years of age or less. The bellicose Russian mavens of the ice, which many would equate to an NHL all-star team (hey, they actually defeated an NHL all-star squad 6–0 last year) will seek to derail the Herb Brooks contingent and send them whining back home like the kid whose toy truck was run over by a bus.

What happened the last time these two teams met? The scene was the most famous arena in the world, Madison Square Garden, three days prior to the commencement of the Lake Placid proceedings. The exhibition purposely arranged by Coach Brooks saw the Soviets dismantle the apparently overmatched USA deputation, 10–3.

So how do our guys defeat the ice hockey Goliath with a litany of superlative adjectives to describe their prowess on ice? Most of the experts expect a five-goal differential in the contest based on the Russians' superior size, team experience, and most importantly, hockey skills. Is there any way that the USA team speed, Jim Craig standing on his head and doing cartwheels on skates, and the encouragement of the faithful US supporters at the arena can maintain a competitive balance tomorrow?

Winning isn't everything, you know. Uh-oh, Herb Brooks just called me an expletive!

Bob read the Sports Chat column and then put down the paper. *Way to go, Kowalski*, he thought to himself. He was procrastinating now. The realization of his requirement to make a decision and call the St. John's athletic director was looming. Ambling over to his desk, he dialed the number.

"This is Bob Murphy. I'd like to accept your offer. I can start following the Monsignor McClancy school year. How about making my first day the Monday after the Fourth of July?"

Good-bye Crusaders. Hello, Redmen.

5

The Al Michaels TV call, as the contest expired, would leave a lasting impression on millions of Americans. Perhaps, only the freedom of fifty-two US citizens held hostage in Iran would have been cause for greater celebration to the serendipitous outcome.

As the final seconds wound down to complete the last of the three twenty-minute periods of the USA 4–3 victory over the Soviets, elation filled the airwaves. "Do you believe in miracles? Yes!"

Sports Chat by Joe Kowalski
February 23, 1980

"Proud to be an American." "Greatest country in the world." "What the hell were you thinking, Tikhonov, but thank you."

The first two quotes were heard repeatedly, in the aftermath of the USA 4–3 triumph over the presumably unassailable Soviets; Initially by eight thousand five hundred spectators at the Lake Placid Field House and then on the streets outside of the arena. American flags were proudly displayed everywhere. I'll explain the final quote, which was mine, by the way, later.

The last time anyone saw tears of joy streaming down my cheeks was when I witnessed the birth of my daughter. That was until yesterday. OK, maybe there was a little moisture when my two best friends married their mates in a dual wedding ceremony three months ago.

It is difficult to convey the feeling of patriotism experienced as time was expiring. Although those of you who watched on TV and had the privilege of hearing Al Michaels conclude his game broadcast just may understand. "Do you believe in miracles? Yes!" will certainly compete with "The Giants win the pennant, the Giants win the pennant" for years to come. Kudos to Michaels.

I was doing OK with the tears until I saw goaltender Jim Craig interacting with his dad. I was cognizant of the fact that his mom had recently passed away and that he and his father had a special bond. Hey, Jim, God bless your mom. Great game, buddy.

OK, speaking of goaltenders, it is time to explain the Joe Kowalski quote from the opening paragraph of this column.

When hockey experts discuss the greatest goalies in the world, regardless of either amateur or professional status, few will omit the name of Vladislav Tretiak from the conversation. Enter the mind of Soviet Coach Victor Tikhonov. The question will be asked for a long, long time. Was he correct in replacing Tretiak with Vladimir Myshkin at the conclusion of the opening period of the game? Did he overreact to the Mark Johnson goal a second before the buzzer had sounded, which knotted the score at 2?

Listen, I had a book published last year, Dopey Bastid, *which was based on foolish sports world decisions by managers, coaches, owners, players, and sportswriters. Guess what? The removal of Tretiak by Tikhonov gives me the ammunition for a chapter in the sequel. There is just no way that one of the best netminders in the world should have been replaced.*

Back to our guys. It would not be possible to tell the story of this unforeseen victory without extending accolades to the USA Captain, Mike Eruzione. The team elder statesman from Winthrop, Massachusetts, and Boston University put our guys on top with the game's final goal midway through the last period. The reaction of his teammates made it appear as if the US had won the gold medal.

Alas, not even the astonishing defeat of the USSR has accomplished that. Sunday afternoon, park yourselves in front of your TV sets and listen to my friend Al Michaels. We have another game to win. Just one more victory over Finland will do it. Watch with your family and friends and root your—off. I'll wager that it will be a most rewarding sentiment that you'll never forget. USA! USA! USA!

On Sunday, February 24, Janet and Bob Murphy and Grace and Lou Marciano once again visited the condo apartment of Susan Kowalski and her daughter, Grace Janet. The girls were preoccupied with the adorable eleven-month-old until the pressure of a 2–1 USA deficit after two periods had Lou up from his chair. "Get in here, girls, and watch the third period. Here, give this little USA flag to Grace Janet. She can wave it in about forty minutes, I feel it."

Phil Verchota, Rob McClanahan, and Mark Johnson all had final-period tallies. Final score: USA 4 – Finland 2. The gold medal in ice hockey was now back in American hands. The Al Michaels's parting line in the victory over the USSR was heard repeatedly in thousands of households across the country; an amalgam of patriotism and downright "just feeling good about life" prevailed.

Do you believe in miracles? Yes.

1980 US Olympic Hockey Team Scoring Summary

PLAYER	AGE	COLLEGE	POSITION	GOALS	ASSISTS	TOT. PTS
NEAL BROTEN	20	MINNESOTA	FORWARD	2	1	3
STEVE CHRISTOFF	21	MINNESOTA	FORWARD	2	1	3
MIKE ERUZIONE (1)	25	BOSTON U	FORWARD	3	2	5
JOHN HARRINGTON	22	MINN-DULUTH	FORWARD	0	5	5
MARK JOHNSON	21	WISCONSIN	FORWARD	5	6	11
ROB McCLANAHAN	22	MINNESOTA	FORWARD	5	3	8
MARK PAVELICH	21	MINN-DULUTH	FORWARD	1	6	7
BUZZ SCHNEIDER (2)	25	MINNESOTA	FORWARD	5	3	8
DAVE SILK	21	BOSTON U	FORWARD	2	3	5
ERIC STROBEL	21	MINNESOTA	FORWARD	1	4	5
PHIL VERCHOTA	22	MINNESOTA	FORWARD	3	2	5
MARK WELLS	21	BOWLING GREEN	FORWARD	2	1	3
BILL BAKER	22	MINNESOTA	DEFENSE	1	0	1
DAVE CHRISTIAN	20	NORTH DAKOTA	DEFENSE	0	8	8
KEN MORROW	22	BOWLING GREEN	DEFENSE	1	2	3
JACK O'CALLAHAN (3)	22	BOSTON U	DEFENSE	0	0	0
MIKE RAMSEY	19	MINNESOTA	DEFENSE	0	2	2
BOB SUTER	22	WISCONSIN	DEFENSE	0	0	0
JIM CRAIG (4)	21	BOSTON U	GOALTENDER			
STEVE JANASZAK	22	MINNESOTA	GOALTENDER			
NOTES:						
	(1) TEAM CAPTAIN					
	(2) ONLY PLAYER FROM THE 1976 US OLYMPIC TEAM					
	(3) INJURED UNTIL MEDAL ROUND GAMES					
	(4) LED ALL GOALTENDERS IN GOALS AGAINST AVG. (2.14) & SAVE % (91.6)					
	TOTAL OF SEVEN GAMES PLAYED					

Many sports enthusiasts forget that, despite the jubilation of the US hockey team after defeating the indomitable USSR squad in 1980, they were still one victory shy of the gold medal. Two days later, on Sunday, February 24, the "Do you believe in miracles?" contingent accomplished that goal. Trailing Finland 2–1 entering the final period, amateur hockey supremacy for the red, white, and blue was achieved. Three unanswered goals were cause for a renewal of the chant "USA! USA! USA!"

CHAPTER VII

ONLY THE GOOD
DIE YOUNG

1

The *New York Daily News* Golf Outing for 1980 was played on Saturday, August 23, at Van Cortland Park. Joe Kowalski, he of Sports Chat column fame, was afforded with the opportunity to have his own foursome for the festivities, which included a nice handout (golf balls, golf shirt, and golf hat) and prizes for "closest to the pin" on all four par 3s, two longest drive holes, and the top three groups with the lowest team scores in the "best ball" format.

The golf gala also provided lovely lasses on golf carts distributing beverages, a stopover hot dog stand after the ninth hole, and a culminating buffet extravaganza with open bar as the awards were distributed.

Joey's guests were his dad, Bob, and Lou; the former, at seventy-two, still sported the lowest handicap of the foursome at fourteen. Bob was the second low handicapper of the Kowalski foursome, carrying a sixteen, while Lou and Joey were each a stroke above Murphy.

"Hey, with my dad hitting the fairway on just about every hole, Bob can let it loose off of the tee without worrying. My irons to the green are my strong point, and damn, Lou can really putt and knows the course well since he played it many times while he went to Manhattan [College]. Shit, we'll be tough in this format."

Joey's dad was full of famous humorous golf quotes and kept the three younger members of his foursome in good humor while traversing the Bronx, New York, course. He always identified who deserved the credit for the sayings.

- "Give me golf clubs, fresh air and a beautiful partner, and you can keep my golf clubs and the fresh air." (Jack Benny)
- "Golf is a good walk spoiled." (Mark Twain)
- "When I'm on a course and it starts to rain and lightning, I hold up my one iron, 'cause I know even God can't hit a one iron." (Lee Trevino)
- "I play in the low '80s. If it's any hotter than that, I won't play." (Joe E. Louis, comedian)
- "If a lot of people gripped a knife and fork like they do a golf club, they'd starve to death." (Sam Snead)
- "For most amateurs, the best wood in their bag is the pencil." (Chi-Chi Rodriguez)
- "My best score ever is 103, but I've only been playing 15 years." (Alex Karras)

Thirty-six teams competed. The Joe Kowalski group was formidable.

- A third-place team finish—10 under par
- Joey's dad and Joey each winning a closest to the pin prize
- Bob capturing one of the two longest drive awards

Lou was tough on himself, not pleased with his contribution to the team. He maintained his wit, however. "Shit, the best two balls I hit all day were when I stepped on a rake in the sand trap."

Lou had a more favorable golf recollection from high school, when he, Joey, and Bob had faced off in a five- dollar bet at the par 3 course at Flushing Meadows Park in Queens. He explained the occurrence to Joey's father.

"So Joey and I are tied as we go to the last hole. Bob is two strokes behind and has virtually no chance of winning. Joey has honors and hits his eight iron [Lou had previously identified that the eight iron was the only club distributed for use in addition to a putter] over the green. He tells us he is going to walk up to find his ball since he is worried about being in the high grass. As he walks to his ball, he drops his umbrella—oh yeah, he was the only pussy to bring one along. Damn, there was only a faint drizzle when we left—just off the back of the green. Bob leaves himself about five feet short of the green, and then I hit my shot, a beautiful low-bouncing pitch off the tee. Hey, the hole was only about seventy-five yards, and there was no trap in the front."

"Yeah right, Lou. That ball was heading toward a spot close to where my ball had landed in the high grass."

Joey felt required to interrupt prior to Lou completing what he had always identified as Lou's fictional "umbrella shot" tale.

"Excuse me, Joey, may I finish telling your dad about the match?" Lou had difficulty in keeping a straight face.

Bob was much more inclined to favor the Joey version of what transpired since his miraculous putt for birdie would have earned him a tie in the match if both Lou and Joey would have bogeyed. He expressed his thoughts on the matter. "Your shot looked as if it would have landed another five to ten yards away, Marciano."

"Just another sore loser who is jealous of my victory, Mr. Kowalski [senior]. So anyway, before I was so rudely interrupted, I was telling you what happened after I hit my marvelous shot. The ball rolled just beyond the back of the green and came to rest in the curved portion of the umbrella handle. The two dipshits were screaming that I should move my ball back twenty feet, complaining that the umbrella handle had caused the ball to come to rest. I invoked a "there's know way to prove that" philosophy and the two bananas had no recourse other than to agree. So the match ended with Joey making bogey and me making par. I won by a stroke over both of the dopey bastards and collected my five dollars from each of the two pathetic souls in front of you."

2

The year 1981 was the year of surname prolongation for Joey, Lou, and Bob. In April, Susan and Joey had their first son, Christopher Joseph Kowalski. The ensuing two months saw the birth of Grace and Lou Marciano's son, Marc Anthony, and Sean David Murphy was the offspring of Janet and Bob. The three best friends soon commenced planning their sons' Little League positions, which would play quarterback, and if any of the three would grow to a height that would exceed guard play in hoops.

Lou expressed his feelings openly as usual. "I hope our boys will grow up to have a special friendship like ours. If they never have birth brothers, they will always have each other."

Joey nodded his head affirmatively.

Bob saw a chance to get back at Lou for years of joking torment. "You pussy. How about growing a dick, Marciano?"

Lou achieved more than an ounce of retribution for Bob's comment when he spoke at Sean David Murphy's christening. His poem for the infant commenced as follows:

> *Sean David is a happy lad, favoring mom, thank God, for looks.*
>
> *And we pray that Janet's brains will emerge, when it's time for him to hit the books.*

*Now if we could only make Bob feel better, 'cause
he is a little sick,*

*For his infant son, Sean David, already has a
bigger . . .*

appendage between his legs.

Joey was particularly amused at the Lou rendition.

Bob was holding back a smile and trying his best to pretend that he was not even the slightest bit impressed. He strode over to his friend as the poem came to a conclusion and whispered in his ear. "Fuck you and the horse you rode in on, Marciano."

The second year of the decade of the eighties also brought other changes to the lifestyle of the threesome. The guys were now heavily involved in pristine work endeavors.

Bob, who thought he would have been seeking to steer the McClancy Crusader ship, vying for a second CHSAA championship, now found his attention on gaining national acclaim for the St. John's baseball program. His mission was to achieve hardball prominence similar to that of his esteemed colleague on the basketball court, Lou Carnesecca. Murphy was also teaching a pre- Revolutionary War American history class.

After fifteen years in the public sector, Lou moved on from his position as the director of engineering and traffic safety with the Long Island town of Babylon. The reputation he garnered in the engineering community enhanced his appeal to private sector firms. After eschewing several offers, he finally accepted a senior vice president position with a leading New England–based engineering firm, Baldwin and Maguire, which sought a manager for its newly founded New York City / Long Island office.

Joey Kowalski was promoted to assistant sports editor of the *New York Daily News*. He continued to write his Sports Chat column twice a week and also focused on developing new concepts to expand the appeal to the newspapers' avid sports enthusiasts. One of his last columns prior to his promotion was indicative of why he was chosen for the role. Joey Kowalski could think out of the box. He also had the benefit of two secret weapons, Lou and Bob, who were constantly offering advice and creative ideas for his column. They suggested that Joey write about the movie that the guys and their spouses had just seen together.

Sports Chat by Joe Kowalski
May 4, 1981

OK, sports fans, I know that we live in the greatest country in the world. That being said, I have a confession to make. The other night I was rooting for Great Britain to defeat the United States in two Olympic races. Heresy, you say. Hey, I got caught up in the freakin' movie Chariots of Fire. *I apologize.*

Listen, before you stone me to death, go see the movie. I realize I can't give away the plot; it will spoil it for you. No suspense, no enjoyment. Well, maybe a few tidbits of information to whet your appetite.

The setting of the movie switches back and forth from England to Scotland before reaching its climax at the 1924 Olympics in Paris. The story, as I have since researched, is loosely based on actual events but like many other films stretches the truth for impact. Hey, who am I to complain about that? I perhaps, ever so slightly, did a taffy pull or two when I wrote my book Dopey Bastid.

The main characters are track stars. Harold Abrahams, a Jew who has enrolled at the University of Cambridge and must overcome anti-Semitism and a class-based superiority of the college masters; and Eric

Liddell, a devout Scottish Christian who runs for the glory of God—"when I run, I feel His pleasure."

In any event, I became enamored of these two guys. Their varied backgrounds, trials and tribulations, and ultimate selection to represent Great Britain as track athletes for the 1924 Olympic Games was intriguing.

I've said enough; go see the movie. You'll love the musical score and the spirit of competition. Let me know who you rooted for during the races. One last thing—I'll give you two to one odds that the movie is nominated for a Best Picture Academy Award.

Yeah, yeah, yeah, shut up about the movie, Kowalski, and tell us about the NBA finals. All right already, here goes.

I was really surprised to see the Lakers go down to the Rockets. I think Moses parted the Red Sea again. This time it was Moses Malone though. It's too bad. With the Celtics coming back from three games to one to defeat last year's champions, the Julius Erving–led Philadelphia 76ers, I was kinda hoping to see Magic and Bird go at it again.

The Boston Celtics, the New York Yankees of the hardwood, are back in the finals. In my youth, I used to get sick of watching Russell, Cousy, Sharman, Heinsohn, the Jones boys, and then Havlicek dominate year after year. As my friend Lou always said, "I'd like to take that freakin' cigar out of Red Auerbach's mouth and shove it . . ." You're right; I left out three words. My dad always told me, though, to give credit where credit is due.

This year, that front court of Boston is extremely formidable, destined to become among the best ever. Bird, McHale, and Parish are pretty awesome. Moses is great. He was the man in the Rockets triumph over the Lakers. Unfortunately for Houston it's time for the happy trails to come to an end. I like the Celtics in five, maybe six games.

Damn, without the Knicks around, I actually find myself rooting for the Celtics! Who woulda thunk it?

3

The Sports Chat columns, although less frequent, remained a *New York Daily News* reader staple. Two losses of life, one sentimental for Joey, and the other tragic, spurred Kowalski discourses.

Sports Chat by Joe Kowalski
January 18, 1982

I doubt that I ever would have become a sportswriter if not for Red Smith. Yes, Walter Wellesley "Red" Smith was most assuredly the genesis of my inspiration.

I remember my first meeting with Mr. Smith vividly. It was 1957 and my two best friends and I were writing our report on Willie Mays, Mickey Mantle, and Duke Snider. It was a joint term paper while we were in the eighth grade. The dad of my friend, Bob Murphy, worked for the Herald Tribune. *He was an acquaintance of Mr. Smith; Red worked as a sportswriter there at the time.*

With some literary guidance from Mr. Smith, my friends and I received an A+ on our report. Well, that was almost twenty-five years ago, and up until his death three days ago, I think I probably thanked him over one thousand times to myself, and thankfully directly to him personally, nearly a dozen. By the way, Mr. Smith always got the highest grades on his articles. When his fingers touched the typewriter keys to generate his distinctive words of wisdom, it always resulted in an A+.

It's difficult for me to express my feelings regarding his greatness as a writer, particularly with regard to baseball. Perhaps boxing and horse racing were not far behind to many a Red Smith fan, but his columns relative to the attributes of New York's Louisville Slugger wielding icons from the Dodgers, Yankees, and New York Giants were undoubtedly the best ever. He always remained humble, however. "There's nothing to writing," said Red. "All you do is sit down at the typewriter and open a vein."

Rather than reading my abortive attempts in written words that pale in comparison to Red Smith's, the best there ever was, I have been given permission to add one of his columns, which remains my all-time favorite. His memories of another truly illustrious and historically relevant man will give you food for thought regarding each.

Thank you Mr. Smith. Rest in peace, my mentor and friend.

October 25, 1972: Unconquerable by Red Smith

In the scene that doesn't fade, the Brooklyn Dodgers are tied with the Phillies in the bottom of the 12th inning. It is 6 p.m. on an October Sunday, but the gloom in Philadelphia's Shibe Park is only due to oncoming evening. The Dodgers, champions-elect in August, have frittered away a lead of 13½ games, and there is bitterness in the dusk of this last day of the 1951 baseball season. Two days ago, the New York Giants drew even with Brooklyn in the pennant race. Two hours ago, the numbers went up on the scoreboard: New York 3, Boston 2. The pennant belongs to the Giants unless the Dodgers can snatch it back.

With two out and the bases full of Phillies, Eddie Waikus smashes a low, malevolent drive toward center field. The ball is a blur passing second base, difficult to follow in the half-light, impossible to catch. Jackie Robinson catches it. He flings himself headlong at right angles to the flight of the ball, for an instant his body is suspended in midair, then somehow the outstretched glove intercepts the ball inches from the ground.

He falls heavily, the crash drives an elbow into his side, he collapses. But the Phillies are out, and the score is still tied.

Now it is the 14th inning. It is too dark to play baseball, but the rules forbid turning on lights for a game begun at 2 o'clock. Pee Wee Reese pops up. So does Duke Snider. Robin Roberts throws a ball and a strike to Robinson. Jackie hits the next pitch upstairs in left field for the run that sets up baseball's most memorable playoff.

That was the day that popped into mind when word came yesterday that Jack Roosevelt Robinson had died at 53. Of all the pictures he left upon memory, the one that will always flash back first shows him stretched at full length in the insubstantial twilight, the unconquerable doing the impossible.

The word for Jackie Robinson is "unconquerable." In the *Boys of Summer*, Roger Kahn sums it up. "In two seasons 1962 and 1965, Maury Wills stole more bases than Robinson did in all of a 10-year career. Ted Williams lifetime batting average, .344, is two points higher than Robinson's best for any season. Robinson never hit 20 home runs in a year, never batted in 125 runs. Stan Musial consistently scored more often. Having said those things, one has not said much because troops of people who were there believe that in his prime Jackie Robinson was a better ballplayer than any of the others."

Another picture comes back. Robinson has taken a lead off first base and he crouches, facing the pitcher, feet fairly wide apart, knees bent, hands held well out from his sides to help him balance, teetering on the balls of his feet. Would he be running? His average was 20 stolen bases a year and Bugs Baer wrote that "John McGraw demanded more than that from the baseball writers."

Yet he was the only base-runner of his time who could bring a game to a stop just by getting on base. When he walked to first, all other action ceased. For Robinson, television introduced the split screen so the viewer at home as well as the fan in the park could watch both the runner on first and the pitcher standing irresolute, wishing he didn't have to throw.

Jackie Robinson established the black man's right to play second base. He fought for the black man's right to a place in the white community, and he never lost sight of that goal. After he left baseball, almost everything he did was directed toward that goal. He was involved in foundation of the Freedom National Banks. He tried to get an insurance company started with black capital and when he died he was head of a construction company building houses for blacks. Years ago a friend, talking of the needs of blacks, said "good schooling comes first."

"No," Jackie said, "housing is the first thing. Unless he's got a home he wants to come back to, it doesn't matter what kind of school he goes to."

There was anger in him and when he was a young man he tended to raise his falsetto voice. "But my demands were modest enough," he said, and he spoke the truth. The very last demand he made publicly was delivered in the mildest of terms during the World Series just concluded. There was a ceremony in Cincinnati saluting him for his work in drug addiction and in his response he mentioned a wish that he could look down to third base and see a black manager on the coaching line.

Seeing him in Cincinnati recalled the Dylan Thomas line that Roger Kahn borrowed for a title. "I see the boys of summer in their ruin." At 53 Jackie was sick of body, white of hair. He had survived one heart attack, he had diabetes and high blood pressure, and he was going blind as a result of retinal bleeding in spite of efforts to cauterize the ruptured blood vessels with laser beams. With him were his wife, Rachel, their son, David, and daughter, Sharon. Everybody was remembering Jack Jr., an addict who beat the heroin habit and died at 24 in an auto accident.

"I've lost the sight in one eye," Jackie told Kahn a day or so earlier, "but they think they can save the other. I've got nothing to complain about."

Joey, Bob, and Lou met at Budd's for a drink after the Joey Kowalski "Red Smith" article appeared in the *Daily News*. Bob was highly complimentary of the Kowalski column as well as his recollection of the acclaimed sportswriter, who had remained friendly with his dad.

"Red certainly gave us a big boost when we did our report. I am pretty sure he thought that Willie had it all over Mickey and Duke."

"Screw you, Murphy."

"You never stop with that Willie Mays crap, do you, Bob?"

The comments of Lou Marciano, who still touted his childhood idol, Mickey Mantle, and Joey Kowalski, he of the Duke Snider admiration society, were bluntly stated.

Sports Chat by Joe Kowalski
March 8, 1982

"Only the Good Die Young." Billy Joel wrote it and sang it; he is truly a great musical talent. I thought about the title of that song when I first heard of the death of John Belushi.

At thirty-three, we have lost one of the Blues Brothers much too soon. My wife, Susan, is a friend of Judy Belushi, having met her in 1974, when she and John were living in New York. John was performing in the National Lampoon Radio Hour. Susan met John several times. "He was a naturally funny guy. You could see his talent was limitless."

Saturday Night Live *revealed his comic multiplicity; Susan and I especially enjoyed his portrayal of Samurai Futaba, Kuldorth from the Coneheads, and Larry Farber, as the husband of the Gilda Radner portrayed Bobbi.*

On the big screen, the guy, in my mind anyway, was even more amazing. My good friends Lou and Bob never miss a chance to watch a rerun of Animal House. The Blues Brothers *will be a classic forever, and his straight role depiction of Ernie Souchak, the Chicago- based newspaper writer who is assigned to research an attractive female scientist studying birds of prey in the Rocky Mountains, revealed his diversity. I guess I was enthralled with that movie because John was a newspaper writer with his own column. So what if it wasn't sports related?*

I have read several of the tributes from his peers. My buddy Lou always says that is what made Mickey Mantle great—his teammates loved him.

His brother, well his Blues Brother anyway, Dan Aykroyd, appeared to be disconsolate after his passing. Likewise, other Saturday Night Live *cast members, including Chevy Chase, Bill Murray, Jane Curtin, and the aforementioned Gilda Radner, only had good things to say about John; his greatness was recognized. John Candy joined in the sorrow of his death and in recognition of his exorbitant talent. I understand that Mork, Robin Williams, was a close friend who also respected Belushi's comic genius.*

I brought up Mickey Mantle before for another reason. Mickey always believed that he would die before he was forty years old and lived his life accordingly, partying hard and often. Belushi had a similar lifestyle. Friends revealed that he would often drink an entire fifth of Jack Daniels in less than five minutes.

Unfortunately, his vices did not cease with alcohol; his death the resultant of combining cocaine and heroin, a speedball.

We lost Red Smith, a great sportswriter, a little over a month ago. He was a friend and mentor. Red was seventy-six years old. Still young, I guess, but at least he led a full life and achieved the plaudits he deserved for his masterful writing accomplishments. John Belushi was much less than half that age, five years younger than I am. He had much more of his limitless talent to share with his fans.

I wish you had stuck in there with us, John. Mickey is still around well past his fortieth birthday; I bet that you could have been too.

Only the good die young?

At the humble abode of Bob and Janet Murphy, the weekend after the passing of John Belushi, the three couples met on a Sunday afternoon. With the girls attentive to the babies, the guys were busting a gut with their memories of the comedic stalwart. The host starts with *The Blues Brothers* movie.

"That scene where the Illinois Nazis show up at Wrigley Field because they think that it is Jake's address cracks me up."

"Asshole. It was Elwood's address on his driver's license, 1060 West Addison, not Jake's." Lou Marciano sought film correctness.

"Bullshit, Marciano, it was Jake," added Bob Murphy.

"Sorry, Bob, Lou is right, it was Elwood." The sportswriter settled another Bob and Lou debate. "Listen, guys, I always liked Jake and Elwood dancing the best, and you two guys are unbelievable at weddings when you mimic them."

"Well thanks, Joey, I am pretty good." And then smiling, Bob said, "Lou isn't bad either."

Later that afternoon the guys discussed the impending fight of Bob Murphy's friend from Huntington, Long Island, Gerry Cooney. His previously scheduled heavyweight championship encounter that month against the undefeated Larry Holmes had to be postponed because of a back injury suffered by Cooney during training.

Bob was confident. "When that fight is rescheduled, Gerry is gong to kick his ass."

Jake (John Belushi, right) and Elwood (Dan Akroyd) performed in January 1980 as the iconic Blues Brothers.

John Belushi died of an accidental overdose on March 5, 1982, at the age of thirty-three. The comedic talent of Belushi was undeniable, spanning his portrayal of *Saturday Night Live* characters, such as Samurai Futaba, Bluto Blutarsky in *Animal House*, and his signature role as Jake Blues. John even proved to be a multidimensional performer with his characterization of a Chicago-based newspaper reporter, Ernie Souchak in the romantic comedy *Continental Divide*.

Belushi was honored with a star on the Hollywood Walk of Fame on April 1, 2004.

4

The Las Vegas trip was planned. Joey Kowalski, Bob Murphy, and Lou Marciano would leave on June 10 for Caesar's Palace. The following evening they would witness the heavyweight championship fight between Larry Holmes and Gerry Cooney.

Joey Kowalski would be covering the fight for the *New York Daily News*. Joey had written several of his Sports Chat columns about Cooney; of particular note were the superlatives attributed to Cooney after his first round KO of Ken Norton at Madison Square Garden in May of the prior year. The fight lasted all of fifty-four seconds.

Bob and Lou were grateful to be receiving tickets to the fight through Joey. They had no problem with paying for their own air fare and hotel accommodations. The three discussed the trip at Budd's. Bob invoked his thoughts on the excursion.

"We'll room together, Marciano, two separate beds, though."

"I was so looking forward to sleeping in the same bed, Murphy."

"Blow me, Lou."

"Well, if we were in the same bed, it would be easier," added Lou, much to the amusement of Joey and the chagrin of Bob.

The review of the records of both Holmes and Cooney ensued. Kowalski had done his research in anticipation of a prefight article on the heavyweight encounter, which began to take on racial overtones. The marketing campaign by the respective managers, who sought to raise public interest by capitalizing on the race card, reaped benefits. Don King, the champion's manager, dubbed Cooney the Great White Hope, alluding to the fact that the challenger would potentially be the first Caucasian to win a heavyweight title since Ingemar Johansson had claimed the throne by a KO of Floyd Patterson some twenty-three years prior.

One of Cooney's managers, Dennis Rappaport, was the equal of Don King in the promotion; assisting in getting Gerry on the cover of *Time* magazine and fostering the Hollywood crowd interest, including Sylvester Stallone.

Joey had handed copies of his investigation for the WBC heavyweight championship bout to Bob and Lou. The tale of the tape included a breakdown of the pugilists' fights—a compelling 39–0 with 29 KOs for the champion and 25–0 and 20 KOs for the challenger, who was the number one contender for the title, a ranking he also held with the World Boxing Association (WBA).

"I really can't say that I don't like Holmes," said Lou Marciano. "He has pretty much dominated the heavyweights since 1978. I wasn't enamored with the pummeling he put on Ali, but I guess he had no choice. Muhammad was just well past his prime. He should never have fought Larry. Gerry has a good shot to beat him though. That left hook of his is awesome. I just wish he used his right hand more."

Bob is supportive of his Irish friend. "Gerry is going to knock him on his ass. I'm going to put some bucks on him. Let's see what the odds are when we get to Vegas."

Joey reminisced about the Robert Murphy KO of Jack Campo when the three were in the eighth grade. "Bob really put a whooping on Jack that day."

5

On June 11, 1982, Joe Kowalski watched in earnest in the sportswriters section of the Caesar's Palace arena while Bob and Lou enjoyed the view from their seats some twenty-five rows from ringside.

After Wilfredo Gomez disposed of Juan Antonio Lopez via a tenth-round KO to retain his WBC super bantamweight title, Bob anxiously awaited his Long Island buddy to step through the ropes. Bob discussed the purse for the pugilistic encounter.

"Ten million bucks, Lou. Gerry will be sitting pretty for a lifetime."

"We'll be witnessing the richest fight ever, Murphy. By the way, how much did you bet that asshole at the bar last night?"

"I took two to one, my five hundred dollars to his one thousand dollars that Gerry knocks him out."

The prefight introductions were somewhat strange: Holmes was introduced first—very peculiar in as much as Larry, the champion, would typically be paid the homage of the latter of the two to be identified. His weight is given as 212½ pounds. Gentleman Gerry Cooney, displaying a shamrock on his trunks and announced at fifteen pounds heavier than Holmes, appeared to have the support of the majority of the thirty-two thousand spectators. Despite the racial overtones of the fight promotion, several ringsiders heard Holmes, the Easton Assassin, proclaiming to the challenger after the two touched gloves, "Let's have a good fight."

Lou was not enamored with the choice of referees.

"Mills Lane is a good ref, but he is too small for the heavyweights. That little shit should stick with middleweights and below. Breaking up those two guys in a clinch will be a chore for him."

Bob looks for humorous glory. "Do you think he tells his wife 'Let's get it on' [the calling card ID of Mills Lane as he requested the fighters to commence fighting] when they get into bed together?"

After a "feeling out" opening round, a second-round knockdown of Cooney from a Holmes's right hand has Bob a little concerned.

"Come on, Gerry, get up and start pounding this guy to the body, and then let me see the left hook."

Two rounds later, Cooney hurt Holmes with a body punch, but the champion had time to recover with the blow striking him just before the conclusion of the round.

"Way to go, Gerry, you hurt him with that punch."

"You're right, Bob, but Cooney has to keep showing him his right hand, and when he jabs, he has to double up. I have the fight even by the way. I gave Gerry the last two rounds and scored the first round even. Holmes gets a 10–8 round for his knockdown in round two."

Rounds 5 through 8 were highly combative, the two heavyweights trading punches in midring. Observers in the surrounding seats felt Cooney had pretty much held his own despite a cut above his left eye from the accurate right hands of the champion.

"Great fight, Bob. It seems as though Gerry may be starting to take it to him."

"Take it to him, my ass, he's going to knock out that shithead."

Lou continued to invoke the wisdom of watching many fights with his dad and brother as a kid. The Friday night fights were a family tradition.

Bob was looking for one thing and one thing only— Cooney to have his hand raised as victor prior to the end of the fifteenth round.

Unfortunately, round 9 saw Cooney visiting the canvass for the second time while his most effective blow was a left hook to the testicles of Holmes. The punch delayed the fight for several minutes and cost Gerry a point on the scorecards.

"Son of a bitch, just when Gerry had it going," lamented Bob. "The knockdown and low blow will really cost him."

Mills Lane continued to warn Cooney about his punches below the belt; in round 11, he invoked a second penalty.

"I want him to knock out Holmes. I don't give a shit about the points," noted Bob.

"Well, Murphy, Victor Valle [Cooney's trainer] is probably telling him he needs a KO to win the fight."

Holmes seemed to have the edge in round 12 and began to land his right hand repeatedly in round 13. Despite a gallant effort, Holmes was just too much for Cooney to overcome. The champion, with a barrage of punches, had Cooney trying to grab the ropes to remain erect. Despite mild protestations from Gerry, Victor Valle entered the ring to protect his fighter from further punishment; the fight was officially stopped at 2:52. The WBC heavyweight championship belt would not be placed around the waist of the Irish, Huntington, Long Island Great White Hope.

Gentleman Gerry was dauntless but second best.

"Gerry put on a good show, Murphy. He has nothing to be ashamed of."

"Yeah, he did. But I am down five hundred dollars and need a few drinks and a good steak. You're buyin.'"

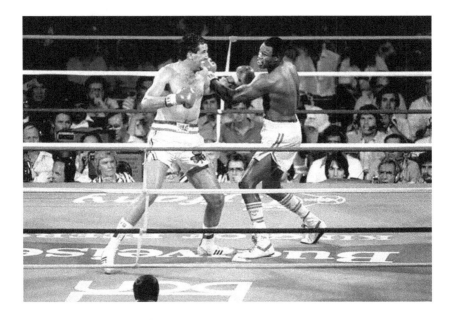

The Great White Hope, Gerry Cooney (left) went toe- to-toe with the champion Larry Holmes in their WBC heavyweight title bout on June 11, 1982. The two fighters, each previously undefeated, waged a highly competitive battle before the gallant challenger eventually succumbed to a barrage of blows from Holmes.

CHAPTER VIII

THE JACKIE AWARD

1

In the fall of 1982, Grace and Lou welcomed their second child, a brother for Marc, their firstborn. Scott Jonathon Marciano weighed in at a whopping nine pounds, four ounces.

"Thank God he doesn't have Lou's schnoz," noted Bob.

"Well, did you see that pecker?" rebutted Lou. "It's bigger than yours, Murphy."

A month later, right before Thanksgiving, Bob and Janet were the parents of a daughter. Gabrielle Murphy, with her reddish blond hair, would be the envy of the boys in next to no time.

"That's it for us," said a radiant Janet Murphy to her husband.

The inseparable couples were now all two-child families; Joey and Susan with a daughter and son, likewise for Bob and Janet but born in reverse order, and two boys for Lou and Grace.

2

In 1976, a special award was created in honor of Jackie Robinson. To many, it was much too long in the making.

The Jackie Award recognized the New York metropolitan area sports media personality or writer who best exemplified the spirit, courage, and determination of Jack Roosevelt Robinson, the Brooklyn Dodger Hall of Fame infielder who had passed away in 1972.

The individuals most closely identified with the origination of the award were Jackie's Dodger teammate, Pee Wee Reese, sportswriter Red Smith, and Howard Cosell.

The festivities for the tribute were held in late March, usually prior to the final four of the NCAA basketball tournament, at the Ritz Carlton Hotel. The emcee for the event since the award's inception was the indomitable Cosell.

The initial award winner was a sportscaster pioneer, Marty Glickman. Many in attendance at the inaugural dinner were educated by Howard Cosell as he expounded on the accomplishments of Glickman; the cognizance of Marty's background as an exemplary athlete in his own right was unbeknownst to the majority.

Glickman was a member of the United States Olympic Team in 1936. A track star at the University of Syracuse, Glickman practiced for two weeks at the site of the Games in Berlin, Germany, in anticipation of running on the 4×100 relay team. In what was an obvious case of anti- Semitism to most, Glickman and teammate Sam Stoller, also a Jew, were removed from the team one day before their scheduled competition. Jesse Owens, a friend of Glickman, was apologetic and protested the move even though he and Ralph Metcalfe were replacements for the Jewish duo. Avery Brundage, chairman of the US Olympic Committee, and Dean Cromwell, assistant US Olympic track coach, were closely associated with the travesty; each was known to be members of America First, an isolationist political movement that attracted American Nazi sympathizers.

Glickman, who also had stints in both professional football and basketball, was more recognizable to the audience relative to his broadcasting, which included twenty-one years as the voice of the New York Knicks and twenty- three seasons at the mike for the New York football Giants and being a host for pre- and postgame shows of the Yankees and Dodgers for over twenty years.

Bob and Lou had been given a copy of the program for the 1983 Jackie Award ceremony. Why? One of the nominees was none other than their best bud, known in the industry as Joe, not Joey, Kowalski.

The two met at Budd's in Jackson Heights several days before the event. Joey was unable to be the third pea in the pod.

Bob was not a happy camper regarding March Madness; he was disconsolate after his alma mater and current employer, St. John's, the number one seed in the east of the NCAA tournament, had been eliminated by Georgia in the regional semifinal.

"I spoke with Little Louie yesterday, Lou. He felt we would make it to the Final Four."

"It would have been great except for the fact that my cousin's squad would have gone up against your team."

Lou alluded to the fact that Jim Valvano, his second cousin and coach of the upstart North Carolina State Wolfpack, miraculously managed to reach the select group of four by advancing as a sixth seed out of the west region. They were now scheduled to play Georgia, who, after disposing of the Redmen, also upset the second seeded team in the east, North Carolina.

"NC State versus North Carolina would have had the whole state in a frenzy, right, Marciano?"

"My cousin would have loved to go up against Dean Smith. He genuinely respects the guy, but a victory over the Tar Heels in the NCAA Tournament would have put his program on the map."

Bob changed the subject and referred to the Jackie Award dinner program. "Glickman always cracked me up when he did the Giant games with Al DeRogatis."

Lou emphatically concurred. "Shit, Murphy, how many times did we turn down the TV audio and just listen to those guys on the radio?"

"You got that right, Lou. How about when he would describe Alex Webster as going for 'a couple of three yards'?"

"What a pisser he was. I can always remember Marv Albert crediting Marty for much of his success as a broadcaster.

Why the hell did he ever leave the Giants to do the Jet games anyway?"

"Yeah, from Big Blue to the shitheads at Shea, Gang Green," said Lou. "By the way, Murphy, did you get your copy of the *Sports Illustrated* swimsuit issue?"

"Of course, Marciano. My girl Cheryl Tiegs is on the cover again. That's her third time, I think."

"She certainly has a great bod and the beauty to go along with it. I kinda like her and Christie Brinkley. She was on the cover three years in a row. I'm sure she makes Billy Joel happy."

"You know what, Lou? We forgot about another hottie. How about Carol Alt, who is going to marry Ronnie Greshner of the Blueshirts. She was on the cover last year."

"You're right, Bob. We should tell Joey to do an article on the girls from the swimsuit issue. It is *Sports Illustrated* isn't it?"

3

Over four hundred people gathered at the 1983 Jackie Award ceremony on the first Friday of spring. The Joey Kowalski table included his mom and dad, his sister and brother-in-law, his better half, Susan, and his two best friends and their spouses, the family-like foursome that Joey had known since his childhood.

Bob and Lou recollected the effort of Joey's sister, Nicole, as they progressed the now famous, at least to themselves, book report on Willie Mays, Mickey Mantle, and Duke Snider.

"We were lucky to also have Nicole doing the review for everything that Joey wrote," observed Lou. "She certainly was a tremendous asset with spelling, grammar, and vocabulary."

Nicole, five years Joey's senior, had a big smile as she proclaimed, "And I knew as much about baseball as you three bozos. My only problem was always having you and Bob checking out my butt."

"Now you've gone too far, Nicole," added Bob. "Maybe you knew the Dodgers as well as Lou and I, but let's not get crazy, sweetheart. And by the way, who says it was just your butt we were checking out?"

Joey supported his big sister. "Listen, Bob, she knew more about the Dodgers than I did because she had those extra years learning from my dad."

"By the way, Nicole, your butt still ain't bad. Don't spank me for saying that, Mrs. Kowalski [Joey's mom]." Nicole didn't have a problem with Lou's humor.

The senior Kowalski acknowledged his son's remarks. "I vividly remember the 1955 World Series, when Podres shut out the Yankees in the seventh game. Nicole was sixteen at the time and had a major crush on him. She told me something like "Don't worry, Dad, my guy Johnny is not going to let one Yankee cross the plate today."

The awards program was then the topic of conversation.

Lou took the lead in eliciting comments regarding the prior year winners. "Bob and I had a great time discussing Marty Glickman last week."

"What was done to Glickman at the '36 Olympics was disgraceful," noted Joey's dad, who then goes on to expound on the events in Berlin.

Lou read off the Jackie winners who followed Glickman. Then Joey, his dad, his brother-in-law (Phil), Bob, and Lou offered their comments. The ladies, except for an occasional interjection from Grace, discussed their children, or in the case of Joey's mom, her grandchildren.

1977 – Red Smith, sportswriter, *New York Times*

"The best baseball sportswriter ever," noted Joey. "I certainly owe any success I have had as a writer to him. He is the reason I wanted to write about sports. I am not sure who knows this but Red was the first sportswriter to win the Pulitzer Prize for commentary."

"When was that?" inquired Phil.

"1975."

1978 – Bill Mazer – WNEW TV, *Sports Extra* show, and sports radio

Bob alluded to the time when he would listen to Mazer in his college years, consistently in amazement of his recall to sport history.

"His nickname wasn't A-Maz-In for nothing."

Joey read from the program notes. "Bill Mazer is recognized as the host of the first sports talk radio show in history, when in 1964, his WNBC AM broadcast aired in March. His knowledge of sports trivia was mind-boggling to many as he continually demonstrated his quick recall to any sports question of his call-in listeners. Mazer also was the author of several sports trivia books, including *Bill Mazer's Amazin' Baseball Book* and *150 Years of Baseball Tales & Trivia*.

1979 – Lindsay Nelson – New York Mets TV broadcaster

Lou commented about the announcer from the New York City baseball team he had always deemed to be inferior.

"I must admit, even though I think the Mets suck and always will, he was an excellent baseball broadcaster. Although where the hell he got those sport jackets from, I'll never know."

Joey added to the conversation. "The year 1978 was his last year with the Metsies. I think he just never got over the stupidity of the Mets trading Seaver in '77."

Joey then solicited input from the others regarding the trade that was viewed in the *Dopey Bastid* category within the Joey Kowalski sports tome of the same name.

Bob reverted to discussing Nelson. "I think he got the award that year because the voters knew he was going to end his tenure with the Mets in New York and head west to do the San Francisco Giant games."

"It certainly wasn't because of his freakin' sports jackets." Guess who.

1980 – Bill White – New York Yankees
TV/radio broadcaster

Bob had high praise for White as a ballplayer. "Well, he started his career in 1956 playing with Willie in the Polo Grounds. Then after the Giants moved to San Francisco, it got a little crowded at first base. Shit, Cepeda came up in '58 and McCovey in '59. White became an all-star after he got traded to the Cardinals."

Lou, his beloved Yankees notwithstanding, rooted for the St. Louis Cardinals in the National League. Of course it had something to do with the name and his semi-infatuation with Stan Musial; his first baseball glove sported the name of the Hall of Famer.

"Bill White was quite the ballplayer. If I wasn't using the Yankee lineup during stickball games, I would be the Cardinals. Stan the Man, Ken Boyer, and Bill White made quite the threesome."

The accolades for White continued through the eyes of Joey and his dad, each noting the defensive acumen of White and comparing him to a Brooklyn Dodger fielding stalwart in his own right, Gil Hodges.

Phil took a turn reading from the program. "Bill White was on the St. Louis Cardinals World Series championship team of 1964, was selected for eight all-star teams, and won the Gold Glove Award at first base seven times. He was one of a select few ballplayers to hit over .300 and have more than one hundred RBIs in three consecutive seasons."

Lou picked up the baton. "I'll never forget his call on the Bucky Dent home run."

Joey read from the program. "Here is the call, guys. Deep to left! Yastrzemski will not get it—it's a home run! A three- run home run for Bucky Dent and the Yankees now lead it by a score of three to two!"

Phil added a footnote that was certainly not supplementary in his recognition for the Jackie. "Bill White was the first African-American to do play-by-play regularly for a Major League sports team."

1981 – Marv Albert – broadcaster New York Knicks and New York Rangers

Perhaps the program offered the best rationale for the Albert selection in 1981. "Many sports enthusiasts believe that Carly Simon was referring to Marv Albert's prowess at the mike when she sang "Nobody Does It Better."

Bob, Lou, and Joey all heartily concurred with the first-line assessment in the Jackie Award handout.

"I'd rather listen to Marv than anyone," noted Joey.

"Bradley from twenty, *yes!*" was a Murphy reaction.

"He was only twenty-six when he first did a Knicks game in 1967. But the best for me was listening to him on radio when the Knicks won game 5 of the finals in 1970. After Reed went down it seemed pretty gloomy, but Marv made you feel that you were at courtside in the Garden as we overcame the Chamberlain, Baylor, and West gang. It was freakin' unbelievable."

Joey smiled at his good friend Lou. "I guess you would have used a different adjective if we were at Budd's, right, Marciano?"

Bob, whose penchant for using language frowned upon by the ladies at the table, easily surpassed Joey and usually even his Italian stallion friend, Lou, just grinned. "It's a good thing you are watching your freakin' language tonight, Marciano."

And then it happened—a comment from one of the ladies, and quite insightful, to say the least. Janet Murphy offers a tidbit relative to the

Carly Simon ballad "Nobody Does It Better." "That was the theme song for the 1977 James Bond film *The Spy Who Loved Me.*"

Bob offered a compliment to his spouse and then decided to hit a home run with the male contingent at the table. "I bet nobody knows who that song was really intended for."

Once again, similar to many episodes in their youth, a huge mistake was made by Murphy—the assumption that he knew a sports trivia answer that Lou did not. When Bob witnessed Lou smiling, he put his hand over his eyes in disbelief.

Joey, who had seen this act countless times before, was convulsing with laughter. "OK, Marciano, give Murphy the answer so we can give you your props, and then have Bob apologize for questioning your knowledge. I assume it had to be an athlete, or you wouldn't know the answer."

"Billy Cannon, LSU, 1959 Heisman Trophy winner."

A quite unhappy Bob Murphy responded, "I wish we were at Budd's, Lou. I'd tell you where to go."

1982 – Art Rust Jr. – Sports Radio WABC

"Art Rust Jr. is a sports trivia expert, noted writer, and creative sports radio host. He reminds many of a previous Jackie Award winner, Bill Mazer, with his uncanny knowledge and memory recall of sporting events that transpired several decades prior."

"The program is right on," noted Bob Murphy. "He knows his shit—er, I mean, stuff."

Lou Marciano cackled at Bob's slip of the tongue. "I remember answering several questions posed by his listeners well before he did, but you are right, Bob, he does know his sh—stuff."

Joey identified the courage of Rust. "His book *Get That Nigger Off the Field* took a lot of guts to write. I recall him taking flak for using that title."

Phil offered insight into the creativity of the award winner. "He really knows his music. I remember listening to one of his shows last month, and he had on a friend of his, Miles Davis. It was refreshing to listen to the integration of sports and harmony."

4

After the appetizers were served, the nominees for the 1983 Jackie were introduced by the emcee for the evening, Howard Cosell. A description of the rationale for their candidacy was expounded on.

1983 Jackie Award Finalists:

Werner Wolf – TV prime time sports anchor – CBS

Entertaining and creative sportscaster best known for his expression "Let's go to the videotape."

Dave Anderson – sportswriter – *New York Times*

1981 winner of the Pulitzer Prize for sports commentary; only the second sportswriter to achieve that honor.

Bob Murphy – TV sportscaster – New York Mets

Met fans love his eternal optimism and his tenure has continued since the inception of the organization.

Joe Kowalski – sportswriter/asst. editor – *New York Daily News*

His Sports Chat column has set a new standard for the profession; author of the sports novel *Dopey Bastid*.

Cosell was highly complimentary of the four and exhibited no favoritism. His final comment did have several attendees muttering, however. "By the way, Joe Kowalski, at thirty-eight, is the youngest finalist we have ever had for this award." Werner Wolf was forty-six, Dave Anderson, fifty-four, and Bob Murphy, fifty-nine.

Susan Kowalski thought if funny that one of the finalists competing for the Jackie Award against her husband was the New York Mets sportscaster with the same name as one of Joey's best friends.

"Remember, Janet, that's not your husband up for the award, root for Joey."

Two guys at a table in the back found it humorous to cast aspersions on Joey Kowalski. The heckling seemed quite inappropriate for the function.

"Kowalski looks like he's about twenty-one, and his column sucks anyway."

"They probably felt that having a kielbasa-breath Polack as a finalist was as good as having a minority."

Ushers at the event were not quick to respond. This did not sit well with two of the individuals at the Joey Kowalski table, Bob Murphy and Lou Marciano. As they nodded to each other and arose from their seats, Joey Kowalski admonished his friends. "Sit down, guys, let it be."

Lou's expression was difficult to ascertain. Somewhere between the impish smile reminiscent of times he would be in prank mode during an eighth-grade class and the "let me at those guys" reaction from sensing that his friend Bob was in trouble outside of Luigi's restaurant some five years before.

"We'll be back in a minute, Joey, no worries."

Bob said nothing, but he certainly was not smiling as he walked in a direct line to the culprits' table. Upon arrival his message was terse. "Would you two assholes care to join my friend and me outside?"

After each "asshole" seemingly impersonated the stammering of Jackie Gleason in a *Honeymooners* episode, their apologetic responses ended any potential for an altercation.

Lou's broad smile upon returning to the table put Joey at ease.

"Bob gave them an offer they couldn't refuse."

Joey's dad was appreciative. "I certainly can see why you three have remained best friends all these years. It always seems that you have each other's back."

Lou expressed the sentiments that Bob was also thinking. "He's our brother, Mr. Kowalski."

From an adjacent table, a young, well-endowed adult female approaches Joey.

"Hi, Mr. Kowalski, my name is Trisha and I am majoring in journalism at Columbia. My goal is to be a sportswriter. I just wanted to tell you how much you have inspired me with your Sports Chat column."

Joey was impressed. "Thank you, Trisha. You know that I also majored in journalism at Columbia, right?

Bob leaned behind his wife, Janet, to offer what he hoped to be a comment that Lou will find humor in. "The old 'I am majoring in journalism at Columbia' routine."

Janet heard Bob's remark. "Would you two just stop. She looks like she has nice qualities about her."

Lou couldn't help himself. "You got that right, Mrs. Murphy. In fact I would say that she has two nice qualities about her."

Bob and Lou got up laughing and identified that they were going to the bar.

Bob inquired, "Who needs a drink?"

Upon returning with the varied beverages, mostly alcoholic, Bob and Lou were amazed that Trisha remained in what Lou described as "ogle over Joey" mode. Bob was grinning from ear to ear since it was evident that Joey was enjoying every phrase of admiration uttered by the attractive lass.

Susan finally interjected. "You are giving him a swollen head, Trisha."

Lou, who now returned to his seat, was smirking as he whispered to Grace, "Yeah, upper and lower."

The superlatives from Ms. Columbia Journalism finally subsided, and Lou was now in game time mode.

"OK, everyone, pick the reason why you think Joey should win this award."

Joey's mom responded instantly. "He is the best son ever. Every mother should be so blessed."

"He has the utmost respect for his profession and his heart and soul are perceived in every Sports Chat column." A proud father succinctly offered his view.

"What sportswriter has a column on the death of John Belushi? He isn't afraid to think outside the box." Nicole's analysis was seconded by her husband, Phil.

"No way, Phil. You have to come up with your own comment, you banana." Lou Marciano frowned upon unimaginative retorts.

"OK, Lou, put me down for the column on Thurman Munson after the plane crash. I didn't even really like Munson, but I had tears in my eyes after I finished that Sports Chat tribute."

Janet Poska Murphy has the floor. "He's intelligent, cute, and Polish. Who could ask for more? But if you really need a specific, I would have to say that his column on *Chariots of Fire* did it for me. Joey even proved to be the movie maven when he predicted the film would win Academy Awards. I think it won four, right? Including Best Picture."

Grace realized that her good friend had left her with a tough act to follow. "Well, Janet hit the bull's eye, but I would certainly add that Joey is just a truly special person, and I am privileged to have him as a friend. I would augment that with his series of articles on the US hockey team in the 1980 Winter Olympics. They were truly opportune and inspiring."

Susan was next at bat. "Wow, you guys should be up at the podium whispering in Howard's ear. I would obviously love to see Joey win the Jackie, but if he doesn't win this year, I know he will soon. He is the best sportswriter in New York. In fact, he's the best in the country and I love him."

Before Bob or Lou had a chance to offer praise to Joey, or more likely relay a comic story about their best friend, Howard Cosell was at the microphone. "And the winner of the 1983 Jackie Award is Joe Kowalski."

Susan jumped out of her chair and hugs her husband. The smile on Joey's mom and dad surpassed the time when their son had won the English medal at St. Joan of Arc during his eighth-grade school year.

Joey's mom, dad, and sister were up out of their chairs, applauding wildly.

Bob just shrugged. "I knew he'd win it."

Lou tried to hide the fact that he has tears in his eyes. "Way to go, Kowalski."

Author's Note: The Jackie Award is fictional

Jackie Roosevelt Robinson was the first ballplayer of color in the Major Leagues. He was twenty-eight years of age when he made his first appearance for the Brooklyn Dodgers on April 15, 1947. His career spanned ten seasons, during which time he became revered as one of the most exciting ballplayers to wear spikes on a baseball diamond. Jackie created havoc for opposing pitchers, often rattling them with exaggerated leads, and stole 197 bases in 227 attempts. Robinson won the NL Rookie of the Year Award in 1947, was an MVP winner in 1949, had a lifetime BA of .311, was a six-time all-star, and in 1962, was inducted into the Hall of Fame. He died on October 24, 1972.

5

The day after the Jackie Award ceremony, the families of Robert Murphy and Lou Marciano gathered at the new home of Joey and Susan Kowalski. The Floral Park colonial, just east of Queens, in Nassau County was a good fit for the Kowalskis, containing four bedrooms and two baths. The den provided the guys with a comfortable setting to watch sporting events while the gals were kibitzing in the large eat-in kitchen. The one-fourth-acre lot was spacious in comparison to the residences in Queens and provided ample area for the backyard play of the six kids.

The NCAA final four encounters were the agenda for the day. Two games would determine the teams who would vie for the national championship.

- Georgia versus North Carolina State and
- Houston versus Louisville

With Lou avidly rooting on his cousin's team, the Wolfpack sought to overcome the Bulldogs. Two Cinderella teams; the number six seed in the west region, NC State, facing off with Georgia, the fourth seed in the east.

Lou knew the matchup would be difficult. The SEC school had defeated both the number one and number two teams in the east, St. John's and North Carolina. In the meanwhile, Jim Valvano's squad was earning a Cardiac Kids moniker, having previously defeated eleventh-seeded Pepperdine by a basket, the third-seeded Rebels of UNLV by a mere point, and in what was their most satisfying triumph in the

Valvano era, at least up to that point in time, a one-point conquest over their archrival from the Atlantic Coast Conference, Virginia, in the west final. The latter university, the number one seed, had featured the College Player of the Year, 7'4" Ralph Sampson.

With Bob and Joey lending support, NC State prevailed 67–60.

The marquee matchup pitted the two top teams in the country, Houston versus Louisville, Phi Slama Jama facing off with the Doctors of Dunk. The overwhelming majority of college basketball experts felt that the winner of this game would become the national champion.

"Damn," observed Lou. "NC State is going to have their hands full opposing either of these schools. My cousin will have to slow the game down to have a chance against either team."

Houston, led by Hakeem Olajuwon, won the show, 94– 81—an entertaining slam dunk contest on the way to the finals.

Two days later Lou watched the final with his wife, Grace. Both Bob and Joey had commitments, the former with St. John's and the latter with the *New York Daily News*.

"Lou, sit down and relax, you are going to have a heart attack."

"Grace, not now, it's 52–52, for shit's sake. I have to concentrate. Jimmy has got to put the ball in Whittenburg's hands, that guy has ice in his veins."

Thirty seconds later, Lou was going nuts. "Put the ball up, Dereck [Whittenburg], there's not much time."

As the thirty-foot shot arched toward the basket, Lou was beside himself. "Son of a bitch, it's short."

Fortunately for NC State, forward Lorenzo Charles, realized it also. As he grabbed the descending basketball in front of the rim, he forcefully slammed it through the hoop just before the buzzer. NC State was the 1983 national champion.

"Jimmmmeeeeee!" Lou hugged Grace as if he were the winning coach. He watched his cousin prancing around like a chicken with his head chopped off. "Not bad, honey. Joey wins the Jackie Award and now Jimmy wins the NCAA title. Friends and family, pretty damn special."

Jim Valvano, coach of the North Carolina State Wolfpack, experienced the jubilation of the 1983 NCAA basketball championship. His hoopsters were dubbed the Cardiac Kids as four of their five victories were by a margin of one or two points. The final victory saw NC State defeat a heavily favored Houston University team lead by Hakeem Olajuwon, on a Lorenzo Charles put back of a long jump shot by star guard Dereck Whittenburg.

Author's Note:

On March 4, 1993, Jim Valvano, dying of cancer, spoke at the ESPY Awards. His heartfelt and meaningful dialogue left a lasting impression on many in the audience; and for that matter, on me personally. Here are a few passages.

- "If you laugh, you think, and you cry, that's a full day."

- "Cancer can take away all of my physical abilities. It cannot touch my mind, It cannot touch my heart, and it cannot touch my soul. And these three things are going to carry on forever."

6

Lou cringed as he read the Sports Chat column of his friend on May 19, 1983. Bob was of similar disposition as he too was an avid fan of the New York Rangers. Joe Kowalski, also a Blueshirt advocate since childhood, had reckoned that his fan base from Long Island deserved to read plaudits about their ice hockey team. The Islanders had defeated the Edmonton Oilers four games to none two nights before for their fourth consecutive Stanley Cup.

Lou shook his head as he perused the article. "The fourth consecutive Stanley Cup triumph for the boys from Long Island, defeating the Wayne Gretzky–led Oilers in four straight. This conclusion certainly did not sit well with Ranger fans, although their second-round four-games- to-two defeat by the Isles may have given the Nassau Coliseum squad their sternest test. Unfortunately, the result will surely lead to an even more boisterous chant of '1940 . . .1940' when the Rangers visit the Island next year."

Bob called Lou that evening. "Kowalski must have gotten a blow job from Potvin. I just couldn't read that article without puking."

"I never thought they would have gotten past Edmonton, Murphy. That freakin' chant will be tough to take next season."

CHAPTER IX

THE KISSING BANDIT

1

"BIG BROTHER IS WATCHING YOU." George Orwell's 1949 political and social science classic novel was finally upon us. The year was 1984.

Susan Kowalski was now teaching part-time at St. John's, a course in twentieth-century literature. She thought it appropriate to spend a day in discussion of *Nineteen Eighty Four*, a compelling narrative that remained one of her favorites. She spent ten minutes just discussing the popularized adjective from the work, *Orwellian*, which describes official deception and secret surveillance.

That evening she was persuasive that Joey should use the adjective in one of his upcoming columns, or at least make reference to the George Orwell fictional account of tyranny.

"C'mon, Joey, it's 1984, be creative, honey."

"I liked *Animal Farm* better."

2

It was now becoming difficult for the entire trio to be able to meet at Budd's to talk sports and commiserate. Joey had moved to Nassau County Long Island; and furthermore, the work and family commitments of all three were obstacles to the assembly. The faces of Bob, Joey, and Lou were no longer considered to be among the regulars of the Jackson Heights establishment. Yet Joey's status as a sportswriter and his occasional references to his two good friends in his Sports Chat column were often a topic of conversation to many patrons.

It was late August. Bob Murphy was a successful college baseball coach, St. John's having gained recognition in the College World Series before succumbing to the eventual runner-up, Texas. Lou Marciano was the principal in charge of several of the highest profile Long Island development projects for his engineering firm, one of which he believed had the potential for him, Joey, and Bob to invest in. Joey continued writing his column several days a week, and his creative ideas as the associate sports editor of the *New York Daily News* received continuous acclamation by the powers that be. The sportswriter was also gushing over a new Met phenom.

"That kid Gooden is just awesome. His fastball and curveball are both unbelievable and he is still not twenty."

"Joey thinks he's got another Koufax to root for," muttered Bob.

"I hate the freakin' Mets but I wish that young right-handed stud was on the Yankees." Lou was never a believer in the philosophy of rooting for all the New York teams.

Joey Kowalski continued to expound on the mound exploits of Dwight Gooden.

"He beat the Dodgers and Valenzuela last night 5–1. Dwight went the distance and gave up five hits and walked only one. He fanned twelve. He would have had a shutout if not for the HR by Scioscia. The Mets are seventy-one and fifty-eight, not too shabby."

"Enough of that Met shit, Kowalski. I think that we are beginning to see the next Pinstripe sensation."

"Hold on, Lou, do you mean Mattingly? He still has a lot to prove."

"My ass, Bob, he's got the perfect swing for Yankee Stadium, and I think after last night's game he's batting .354."

Joey reentered the conversation. "It appears as if we have two top guys at first base in the Big Apple. Mattingly is good, but he has to take a backseat to Hernandez with the glove."

"You haven't seen him enough Joey," added Lou. "He is as smooth as silk with that first baseman mitt."

"Enough about baseball, the real man's sport is about to begin." Bob had lost some of his passion for America's pastime as played by the professionals. Willie had retired over a decade prior, and his principal baseball concern was now his St. John's Redmen squad. Pro football had become his professional sport of choice, particularly the local team in blue with its rich NFL heritage.

"I'm ready for the Giants to become a contender again. I like Parcells as a coach, Simms is ready for a breakout season, and LT is already one of the best defensive players in football."

"I hope you're right, Murphy. I think it's time for a Sports Chat column on Big Blue," added Joey."

Lou never had a problem discussing his favorite football team. "From your lips to Wellington Mara's ears, Bob, and you should definitely write about the G-men, Joey. By the way, guys, are we going to the first home game?"

Bob Murphy was on target relative to his prognostication regarding the Giants. The 1984 team rebounded from a three-win season to post a record of 9–7 and reach the playoffs. Phil Simms passed for over four thousand yards.

Bob, Lou, and Joey also received an early Christmas present when the Giants, as a 4½-point underdog, defeated the Los Angeles Rams in the wild card game on the road 16–13. Unfortunately, their West Coast fortunes were not as encouraging the following week, succumbing to the eventual Super Bowl champions, the San Francisco 49ers, 21–10.

"Hey it was 14–10 after Carson intercepted Montana and went in for a score. We were twelve-point underdogs, I should have bet." Bob was pretty well satisfied with the progress of the team. "We are getting close, guys. We should contend for the whole ball of wax next year."

3

"C'mon, Joey, what could be more important in the world of sports than that?"

"Lou's right, Kowalski. It's definitely time to resurrect some stories about Willie and Mickey."

"All right, you guys, I'll do it."

Joey was in agreement that the reinstatement of Willie Mays and Mickey Mantle by Peter Ueberroth, Major League Baseball Commissioner, was worth a Sports Chat column.

"You have to, Joey. That asshole, Kuhn, should have had his nuts chopped off. You just don't ban the best center fielder of all time."

Lou Marciano, knowing full well that his friend Bob Murphy was alluding to his own childhood idol, Willie Mays, offered his rebuttal. "Nice of you to talk about Mickey that way, Bob. He was sorely missed at Yankee Stadium."

"Blow me, Lou. You know who I was referring to."

"We'll never resolve that argument, Murphy. Let's just agree that Kuhn was a dickhead who thought he could play God. I could never see the rationale. There's no professional sports team betting in Atlantic City. Now if that was the case and they were betting on baseball games, I would have concurred with his thinking. Way to be Joey. Make sure you put Kuhn in his place when you present the information."

"I will, Lou. Ueberroth sees the big picture. If you are going to promote the game, it's definitely much better with Willie and Mickey in the fold."

Two days later a Sports Chat column appeared in the *New York Daily News* that discussed the reinstatements of Willie Mays and Mickey Mantle to baseball.

The history of the ban was reviewed. In 1980, Willie Mays had taken a public relations position at the Bally's Park Place Hotel in Atlantic City. Mickey had likewise followed suit, with employment from the Claridge in 1983. The promotion of gambling was frowned upon by the commissioner at the time, Bowie Kuhn, who suspended each Hall of Fame icon. On March 18, 1985, the new commissioner, Peter Ueberroth, lifted the ban.

Lou was ecstatic to see his idol return.

"Old-Timers' Day at the stadium will be an event again. Without number 7, it just wasn't the same. I'll bet the Mick will be at opening day at the big ballpark in the Bronx. He hasn't been there since August 1982. Shit, guys, I was just thinkin'. My Mickey Mantle autographed baseball that my Uncle Vin had gotten for me will be twenty-five years old next year. I am saving it for my sons."

Author's Note: The photo above depicts Mickey Mantle (right) preparing to sign a baseball held my Uncle Vin. It was 1961 and the ball remains in my possession. I have it encased and displayed on the mantle (fitting right) above my fireplace. "To Louis, best wishes"— signed by Mickey Mantle.

4

The 1985 NBA draft lottery proved to be noteworthy for one of the great New York Knickerbockers of all time, Dave DeBusschere. The former star forward from the Knicks championship teams of 1970 and 1973 now held the position of general manager for the Madison Square Garden hoopsters and represented the team for the occasion.

DeBusschere and every other lottery team had one prize in mind that day and wondered if the closely scrutinized NBA-sanctioned outcome would be a Vegas jackpot for their franchise. The last team standing, the officially designated winner of the first pick in the draft, would reap the reward of selecting the most dominant player in amateur basketball. In this case the choice was obvious to the basketball mavens heard on TV or radio or read in the newspapers around the country. The unanimous choice for all concerned was the center for the University of Georgetown, Patrick Ewing.

Upon hearing the commissioner identify that the only other team left in the running for number one, the Indiana Pacers, were awarded the second pick in the lottery selection process, Dave knew he had his man. His elation was reminiscent of the glorious initial championship of the Knicks in 1970 when he celebrated with Reed, Frazier, Bradley, and Barnett.

Joey Kowalski, watching the TV with immense anticipation, knew he had the making of another sports commentary in the *New York Daily News*. He felt that he would also add a few paragraphs on the selection of the Portland Trail Blazers a year earlier.

He recalled his buddy Lou calling the Portland franchise a bunch of dopey bastards for bypassing Michael Jordan with the second overall pick in 1984 because they wanted a big man, and their sought-after center, Hakeem Olajuwon, was taken with the first pick of the draft by the Houston Rockets. The Trail Blazers reasoned that their number one pick the previous year, Clyde Drexler, filled their need at the shooting guard position, and that Sam Bowie, out of Kentucky, would provide the rudimentary "big man in the middle" stability for years to come.

"You should draft for talent, not need," observed Lou. "Jordan is going to be a perennial all-star, you just don't pass on a guy with his multidimensional skills."

Joey sought the input of Lou and Bob on what would most certainly be the selection of Ewing by the Knicks.

The former had only one observation: "Let's hope that Bernard heals quickly: Ewing and King would forge the basis for another Knick championship."

The latter, with a second highly favorable response of his own, said, "Holy shit, Joey, that bastard gave my Johnies fits in the Big East. I'm glad he is going to be on our team now. I know that Little Louie feels that he will be dynamic in the pros at both ends of the court. Carnesecca thinks that very few guys will be able to guard him one on one and that his shot-blocking ability will transcend to the professional game."

The following week, as the comrades discussed the potential for Patrick Ewing to come to the Big Apple, Lou related his story of watching the NCAA championship game with his friends, the Snider brothers, each a graduate of Villanova.

"The two of them were whooping it up the whole night. I told them that the only reason they pulled the upset over Georgetown was because they had an Italian coach."

"Yeah right, Lou. Rollie Massimino was a real freakin' inspiration. What did he tell the Nova players? Don't drive the lane and get your shots blocked by Ewing. Just stay outside and shoot jumpers, but make sure you shoot at a 70 percent clip."

"That's right, Bob, Italian foresight."

5

The gathering at the household of Lou and Grace Marciano to watch the NFC divisional playoff game between the Giants and Bears on January 5, 1986, was enthusiastically welcomed by Robert Murphy and Joey Kowalski. Lou had informed the two that his mother, Rose Marciano, would be cooking. Their memories of the many Italian delights they were blessed to partake in as teenagers were vivid and each was salivating in anticipation.

The three-story, three-family brick edifice on Eighty-Third Street in Jackson Heights continued to be home for Lou Marciano. He, along with his wife (Grace) and their two young sons, occupied the second-floor apartment of the home. Lou was hoping to sell the house and move to Long Island but not until he was able to convince his mom and dad, who remained in the first-floor dwelling of Lou's youth, to also head east and move into one of the senior housing complexes.

The guys were enthusiastically rooting for the Giants but became momentarily disheartened as the swirling winds at Soldier Field wreaked havoc on the New York Giant punter, Sean Landeta. His feeble attempt to limit the field position of the Bears was uninspiring, to say the least. Landeta reminded Lou of the many batters he witnessed flailing away at a Ron Guidry slider; only Sean missed a pigskin with his foot, not a stitched rawhide enclosed sphere with his bat.

"Son of a bitch Sean, it's not that fuckin' windy, you bumbling dickhead."

"First 1963 and now this shit. Screw the Bears and screw the windy city."

"Take it easy, guys, it's only 7–0, we can still take care of business."

The respective comments of Bob, Lou, and Joey were somewhat typical of the trio of pals. Joey, the only amigo who refrained from vulgarity, was also heard in a more mellifluous tone than his Irish and Italian comrades.

Fortunately, the decibel level of Bob's and Lou's remarks, as they watched the Bears' Shaun Gale waltz into the end zone from a mere five yards away to gain the early advantage in the game, had no impact on the children of the three friends; they all were being entertained by Lou's dad, Al Marciano, on the first floor.

Lou Marciano was incensed with the ease of the Bears' touchdown. He became further exasperated as he recollected the Giant-Bear encounter some twenty-two years prior.

"It was a lot colder and almost as windy in the 1963 championship game. There is no freakin' way we should have lost that game."

Joey concurred. "I thought we had a touchdown on that Tittle pass to Shofner. That would have given us the victory."

"As I recall, our only touchdown that day came on a Y. A. pass to Gifford. But enough about 1963, we have a game to win today. I'll admit that the Bear defense is awesome, but I think that Simms can make some throws down the middle to Bavaro, and Morris has a chance to break one on them." An insightful Bob Murphy sports analogy without profanity was unusual.

A tempestuous Lou Marciano rebuttal ensued. "Buddy Ryan and the forty-six defense my ass. LT has to put McMahon on his butt a few times and if we can keep Payton under wraps, we can beat these bastards."

"Walter Payton is a great running back. He's the only guy on that team I like." The following Tuesday the words of Joey Kowalski were repeated in his Sports Chat column. An excerpt from the pragmatic column, rife with superlatives, was indicative of the thoughts of the sportswriter.

The voluble Buddy Ryan saw his forty-six defense contain the Giants, sacking Phil Simms six times and limiting running back Joe Morris to thirty-two yards on twelve carries.

The sixteen-miles-per-hour winds at Soldier Field, which partnered with a windchill temperature of three degrees, were also limiting factors in the performance of Simms. Although throwing for a little over two hundred yards, the Giant QB was stifled, completing only fourteen of thirty-five passes.

Middle linebacker Mike Singletary and his Chicago Bear pals are most certainly a force to be reckoned with—a defensive contingent that also includes the likes of all-pro defensive end Richard Dent and a Lawrence Taylor–like Wilbur Marshall. Don't be offended, Giant fans; I said "Lawrence Taylor–like"—there is only one number 56.

Perhaps the Bear defense failed to make professional football aficionados forget the dominance of the Pittsburgh Steelers defensive eleven of the mid to late seventies. Yet you can't take umbrage with a squad that shuts out its opponent.

On the offensive side of the ball, the Bears were able to be successful in the air and on the ground against a Giant defense, which many New Yorkers may have felt was the equal of Chicago's; the optimism is a reflection of their regal performance in the wild card game the previous week against the Joe Montana / Jerry Rice deputation from the West Coast. Jim McMahon passed for 216 yards and two TDs; Walter Payton was seven yards short of the century mark on twenty-seven carries.

The cockiness of the Bears has fashioned a love-hate feeling among NFL fans regarding the Windy City boys. I know that the remarks of my buddies, Lou and Bob, about the Mike Ditka–led squad, would not be, with apologies to the New York Times, fit to print. That being said, I do find myself rooting for Walter Payton. When I think of the great running backs of all time, Jim Brown notwithstanding, Walter may be the best.

Through this regular season, Payton has played in 162 games. Since his rookie season of 1975, the Chicago Bear ultratalented halfback carried the pigskin from scrimmage 3371 times and has gained 14,860 yards for an average yard per carry of 4.41. Walter has 98 rushing TDs. His 5'10", 200-pound frame certainly belies the power of his impact to would-be tacklers. His pure unabated tenacity every time he accepts a handoff or pitchout from the QB presents Mr. Sabol and NFL films with a continuous weekly highlight reel. The nickname Sweetness is not a connotation that would come to mind to opponents faced with the task of terminating his downfield progress.

Payton is the consummate football player, his efficiency not concluding with his prowess as a ballcarrier. He has caught 422 passes for almost 3,600 yards, entering the end zone on another eleven occasions. He is a ferocious blocker, particularly when it comes time to protect his QB. I would wager that Jim McMahon thanks Walter often.

Yeah, Jim Brown aside, I would venture to say that Payton is the best ever.

6

The final round of the 1986 Masters, the fiftieth of such event, was played on April 13.

With the girls Susan, Grace, and Janet taking all the kids to the Bronx Zoo for the afternoon, Lou and Bob joined Joey and his dad to watch the Major thought of as the most prominent of the four by Joey's father. Mr. Kowalski was somewhat of a golf historian.

"To me the mere fact that the Masters is always played on the same course, Augusta, makes it the best. A scenic eighteen holes, which is a true test and rarely won by anyone not considered to be one of the elite."

The axiomatic statement is supported by Lou. "You have my vote Mr. Kowalski."

"Who do you like to win, Mr. Kowalski?" inquired Bob Murphy.

"I bet I know who my father wants to win. Although I am not sure who he thinks will wear the green jacket this year."

"Well, boys, Joey is aware of my feelings for Jack Nicklaus, but he is four strokes back with a myriad of excellent golfers to pass. If I was a betting man and you gave me only one guy, I'd take Ballesteros. He has won the Masters twice already and just seems to have the resolve to win the Majors."

Lou suggested that the four make it interesting. "How about five bucks a man? Everyone selecting two golfers? We should be able to pick the winner with eight shots at it. Mr. Kowalski can have his first pick, Seve, now you go, Joey. Bob will select third and I'll go last. Then we will reverse the order for the second pick."

The picks were all from the top golfers on the leader board after third-round play. This is the way it looked after Saturday.

- Greg Norman - 6
- Seve Ballesteros - 5
- Bernard Langer - 5
- Donnie Hammond - 5
- Nick Price - 5
- Tsuneyuki Nakajima - 4
- Tom Kite - 4
- Tom Watson - 4
- David Edwards - 2
- Gary Koch - 2
- Sandy Lyle - 2
- Mark McCumber - 2
- Jack Nicklaus - 2
- Corey Pavin - 2
- Bob Tway - 2

The golfers chosen for the exorbitant fifteen-dollar profit to be won by the winner were as follows (note that the number in parentheses reflects when the golfer was selected):

- Mr. Kowalski: Seve Ballesteros (1), Bob Tway (8)
- Joey: Greg Norman (2), Tom Kite (7)
- Bob: Nick Price (3), Jack Nicklaus (6)
- Lou: Bernard Langer (4), Tom Watson (5)

"You stole Nicklaus on me, Bob, I like your picks."

"I've always rooted for the Golden Bear, Mr. Kowalski."

Joey had picked two guys who had never worn the green jacket. Lou chose two golfers who had donned the verdant apparel before: Langer, the previous year, and Watson, a two-time winner.

The afternoon was spent with pleasantries amongst the four. Lou was privately sentimental. He was in awe of the respect shown by Joey to his dad, always striving to put his own father on a similar pedestal. *Family and friends*, he thought to himself.

The tournament effectively came down to a battle among four players.

"Shit, it looks like I may be the only guy without a dog in the fight," proclaimed Lou with the event winding down.

For all practical purposes it appeared likely that the 1986 Masters would be won by Ballesteros, Norman, Kite, or Nicklaus.

Nicklaus was several pairings ahead of the others as he approached the sixteenth tee. His birdie on fifteen had given his contingent of fans a glimmer of hope that a sixth green jacket may be in the offing. Another Nicklaus birdie, after a brilliant iron to within three feet of the pin, had the senior Kowalski exclaiming, "I know I don't have him but I want Jack to win this."

Ballesteros, the leader after fourteen holes, was in prime position to go for the par five fifteenth green on his second shot; visions of a third eagle for the day were prevalent as he surveyed his targeted landing area. Unfortunately for the flamboyant Spaniard, a pull hook sent his golf ball into the water. A bogey by Seve now had Nicklaus tied with him for the top spot on the leader board.

Greg Norman had been left for the morgue after a double bogey on the tenth hole. Birdies on the fourteenth, fifteenth, and sixteenth, however, placed the Aussie, the third-round leader, back within one shot of the pinnacle.

The thirty-six-year-old Kite was an eight-time winner on the PGA Tour. He always appeared to be steady and capable of maintaining his composure. He stayed in contention throughout the afternoon. Most golf experts predicted that a victory in a Major would just be a matter of time; but would it be in 1986? Well, a birdie on the fifteenth put Kite in a three-way tie for the lead with Ballesteros and Nicklaus.

Jack Nicklaus had last won at Augusta in 1975. The forty- six-year-old was seeking to become the oldest winner of the prestigious tournament. In fact, a first-place finish would make him the second oldest winner of any Major event—Julius Boros captured the 1968 PGA at the age of forty-eight.

After a wayward drive on the seventeenth hole, Nicklaus recovered with an iron to within eighteen feet of the cup. Then, in what seemed an eternity, the long deliberation of the five-time winner paid off; Jack holed the putt and now had the outright lead.

The support at the Kowalski household was all encompassing. You would not have been able to tell which of the four five-dollar bettors had selected the Golden Bear.

"I think he is the greatest of all time," noted Mr. Kowalski.

"Get ready to cough up your five bucks gentlemen," uttered Bob.

Not so fast, everybody. Greg Norman, after badly hooking his tee shot off the tee, miraculously placed his second shot between two pine trees to within Yogi Berra distance. This is a Louism as Lou Marciano often alluded to the jersey number of one of his favorite Hall of Fame Yankees to describe almost anything that required a one digit numeral—in this case, eight feet. Norman sank the putt for his fourth straight birdie. Score tied!

After Nicklaus finished his round with a two-putt par on the eighteenth, he waited for Kite and Norman to determine his fate.

Would there be a playoff?

Kite put himself in position to join Nicklaus as the leader in the clubhouse, leaving himself with twelve feet for birdie. However, it was not to be. The winner of the '86 Masters would be either Jack Nicklaus or Greg Norman.

"Joey, how about another Budweiser, you shithead?"

"How about doubling the bet, Joey?"

Lou Marciano was thirsty. Bob Murphy sought a Nicklaus over Norman outcome.

"Don't bet against Jack, son." The wisdom of a father?

Norman's drive on the last hole was described with the much overused *perfect* by the commentators.

"Why do all the golf announcers insist on using that fu—I mean, freakin' word all the time? No golf shot is perfect unless it goes into the fuckin' hole. Damn, sorry, Mr. Kowalski, I couldn't hold that one in."

"You are right, Lou," noted Bob Murphy. "It pisses me off too." Of course Bob was even more upset by the fact that Norman had now placed himself in prime position to cost him the fifteen-dollar prize and, more importantly, bragging rights.

Uh-oh, the approach shot of the talented Aussie was hit into the spectators. His third shot recovered to fifteen feet from the pin and a chance for par. As Nicklaus looked on, Norman's putt was not, by Lou's definition, perfect.

There would be no playoff. Jack Nicklaus was the winner of the Masters for the sixth time.

"That will teach you guys not to bet against me."

"Do you mind, Mr. Kowalski?"

"Just one more for the day, I promise."

"Screw you, Murphy!"

In 1986, Jack Nicklaus, at age forty-six, became the oldest player to win the Masters. Entering the final round, the Golden Bear trailed Greg Norman by four strokes and Seve Ballesteros by three. The photo above depicts Nicklaus sinking a critical eighteen-foot putt on the seventeenth hole, which propelled him to a record sixth green jacket.

7

Lou Marciano sat with his father to watch the Yankees play the California Angels on August 25. The televised encounter started early enough to allow his two sons to watch the first inning. Both boys requested to 'just watch Don Mattingly hit one time.'

Al Marciano loved his grandsons and was often seen in the driveway playing catch with Marc, the five-year-old, Scott, soon to be four, or both.

"You are bringing the boys up right, Lou. Nothing better than Yankee baseball. Too bad they couldn't get to see Joe D."

"You're right, Pop, and of course you can add the Mick to that statement also."

The Yankees entered the contest, having lost their last two to the Athletics, and now stood nine games over the .500 mark at 67–58, six games behind the Red Sox. Lou Piniella, the Yankee manager, was hopeful that Joe Niekro would afford the opportunity to commence a substantial winning streak.

The Angels didn't score in the top of the first. The boys were now getting excited. Marc held a bat in his hands as he asked, "Mattingly is up third, right, Dad?"

Ricky Henderson, Willie Randolph, Don Mattingly, and Dave Winfield were the first four hitters in the lineup.

"What do you think, Pop? I believe that in 1951, Stengel had Rizzuto, Mantle, Di Maggio, and Berra hitting in the top four spots for some games. I could be wrong, though, I mean I was only seven. It's just funny to me, three Italians and the Mick."

"Stengel liked to hit Woodling third a lot, Lou. That pushed DiMag to fourth and Yogi to fifth."

"C'mon, Daddy." Marc beckoned as he took practice swings with his Louisville slugger. "It's time to watch Donny hit."

With Mattingly at the plate with one out and Willie Randolph on first, Lou and his father were talking casually when they were interrupted by the giggles of Marc and Scott.

"Look at the lady, Daddy," uttered Scott, Lou's younger boy.

Moving past Angel catcher Bob Boone and the home plate umpire was a buxom blonde seeking the affections of Mattingly.

The vocabulary of Al Marciano vividly described the attributes of the female viewed on the TV screen. Fortunately for his two grandsons, the portrayal was in Italian.

Lou Marciano, understanding the gist of his father's words, laughed hysterically—so loud in fact that his mother, Rose, came into the living room where three generations of Marciano males watched the game.

Later that evening, after putting the boys to bed, Lou spoke to his attractive better half.

"It was, Morganna, Grace, you know, the Kissing Bandit. She has the biggest set of tits that I have ever seen. The expression on my dad's face was priceless. Then he started extolling her virtues in Italian. It was hilarious, hon, although I didn't quite understand everything he said. You would have since you speak and comprehend the language better than I. You know what? I have to call Joey and tell him to write an article about her. Damn, it must have been fifteen years ago that she came on the scene. I think her first episode in the baseball world limelight was with Pete Rose. By the way, honey, what is the largest bra size you have ever heard of?"

"What's this infatuation with breasts, Lou? Aren't mine sufficient for you?"

"Perfect, my love. More than a handful is superfluous anyway."

Much to Lou's chagrin, his attempt to cop a little feel was thwarted. "Save it for Morganna, Lou. And by the way, you can use your hand for anything else you may require tonight."

8

Lou Marciano survived the transgression of obsession with the bosom of Morganna. Grace kidded about it with Susan and Janet the following day.

"There was no way he was getting a shot at my nipples last night though."

Susan and Janet found the comment of their girlfriend entertaining. Each had their own thoughts on the Kissing Bandit topic.

"Well, Lou asked Joey to write a column about her and I told him to forget about it. In fact, I had a similar reaction to Grace and asked him what he thought about my pair."

"Bob reminded me that he had dated Cynthia. Remember her? She was Dolly Parton–like in her own right. Bob pretended that he didn't care about the size of a woman's breasts. I said, 'Yeah right, who the hell are you kidding?'"

Despite the warning from his spouse, Joey Kowalski was curious about the Kissing Bandit and did some research. A few facts about Morganna Roberts, who was now thirty- nine, struck him as particularly humorous and became themes for conversations with his two best friends.

On the phone with Lou that evening he identified a few.

"She has been quoted as saying that her measurements are 60–23–39. One writer used the phrase that Morganna makes Dolly Parton look 'developmentally delayed.' The best story I read though was when her attorney was defending her in court for jumping onto the playing field in Houston. The lawyer told the judge something to the effect of 'Listen, Your Honor, Ms. Roberts is 112 pounds and has a 15-pound chest. When she leaned over the rail to get a foul ball, gravity took its toll.'"

Despondent Yankee fans, having lost two games in a row, got a boost from an unexpected source on August 25, 1986. As Don Mattingly was batting in the bottom of the first inning at Yankee Stadium, thirty-one thousand fans delighted at the sight of the Kissing Bandit, seeking to plant a "wet one" on the all-star first baseman. The buxom-lovely Morganna Roberts was acknowledged by one sportswriter to make Dolly Parton look "developmentally delayed."

CHAPTER X

IT AIN'T OVER UNTIL . . .

1

Sports Chat by Joe Kowalski
October 7, 1986

Our Metsies open up at the Astrodome tomorrow. Are you ready?

I guess that maybe the phrase "our Metsies" is inappropriate; it makes me look more like a fan than a sports reporter. You know what, the hell with it, I am a Mets fan and you all know it.

This is an exciting time for all of us who grew up watching the Brooklyn Dodgers, my team as a youth, and the New York Giants. New York lost those storied franchises at the end of the 1957 season but were rejuvenated at the arrival of the Mets in 1962.

The Metropolitans, good thing that the Mets became the adopted nickname, donned the colors of their National League predecessors, the Dodgers and Giants, blue and orange. Those two teams were intertwined in the fabric of New York, and many a baseball fan sobbed like a three-year-old who had been separated from his mommy when they abandoned the Big Apple and headed to the West Coast.

I was thirteen at the time and, along with one of my best buddies, a New York Giant fan, had a feeling of desertion. What, no Ebbets Field next year? How am I going to get to see the Duke play?

Of course, my buddy lamented the fact that Willie would not be patrolling center field in the Polo Grounds. We were envious that our other best friend still had Mickey to root for.

Then came 1969. It was a glorious year for the Mets. They had this city in an uproar. Unbelievably, we were the best team in New York. The once-proud Bronx Bombers were second fiddle to our Mets. Our boys sat on the throne for a while, even giving us an "almost" in 1973 before succumbing to Oakland.

Gradually, our guys from Flushing began to fade. Damn, incredulously we even traded the best player in the history of the franchise. To make it worse, we were back in the New York City second row as those Pinstripe guys with the blue caps won their twenty-first and twenty-second championships in 1977 and 1978. Wow, I used the word we three times in the last two sentences.

Who cares, because, you know what, we're back, baby! One hundred and three victories for our Davey Johnson– led club, almost 2.8 million fannies in the Shea Stadium seats this season, and we can play Abner Doubleday's game as well as anyone in either League.

Hey, we've got Doc, Ron, Bobby, and Sid as starters; and Roger and Jesse out of the pen. Oh sorry, that's Gooden, Darling, Ojeda, Fernandez, McDowell, and Orosco for anyone not familiar with my team.

Keith Hernandez and Gary Carter are both consummate professionals; they have different ways of expressing themselves maybe, but each guy is a leader and can hit and field. Daryl Strawberry is a young star who has potential greatness in him.

Can you tell I'm excited? This just feels the way it should in this city, for me anyway.

Even my football team is excelling. The Giants are 5–1 and just beat those damn Eagles 35–3 on Sunday. Peeking into my crystal ball shows glimpses of what appears to be a Super Bowl on the horizon. OK, OK, OK, I'm sorry; I didn't mean to jinx Big Blue.

Back to our boys on the baseball diamond. Shea Stadium has been rocking again, and Met fans will be in a frenzy come game 3 against the Astros when they eventually return home.

The Kowalski prediction is the Mets in five games.

Can you say World Series?

"What a crock of shit, Kowalski. I felt like puking after reading that column."

"Too bad, Marciano. It's Mets time now."

2

Sports Chat by Joe Kowalski
October 16, 1986

"It ain't over until it's over."

Yogi, you're not kiddin'. No truer words have ever been spoken in the world of sports than the innocuous yet sometimes prophetic statement of one Lawrence Peter "Yogi" Berra.

Even the most loyal Met fans were dubious that the Mets could prevent the Astros from tying their National League championship series at three games apiece as the ninth inning commenced yesterday at the Astrodome.

Bob Knepper seemingly had the number of the Met hitters. After eight innings, the Astro left-hander had surrendered a mere two hits and was shutting out the Mets. The three- run Astro advantage appeared insurmountable on this day.

Then a glimmer of hope—a leadoff triple by Len Dykstra followed by a Mookie Wilson single got us on the board. After Mitchell grounded out to third and Wilson advanced one base, my wife was screaming, "Let's keep it going, Keith." Hernandez obliged as he doubled, cutting the Houston lead to a single run. I was gleeful as I observed the guy who had impersonated the indomitable Sandy Koufax for eight innings, walking off the mound.

"We can do it, c'mon, Gary," implored my better half. Carter walked; runners were now on first and second with one out.

As Daryl Strawberry strode to the plate, I was out of my chair and speaking to my beautiful wife. "I love Daryl, Susan, but I wish Duke was at the plate." I was satisfied, however, after Strawberry also walked, loading the bases.

As Keith Hernandez crossed home plate with the tying run, a sigh of relief pervaded my being. "Way to go, Ray, a sacrifice fly works for me, at least it ain't over." The thank you was for Ray Knight.

The score remained at 3–3 as the Mets batted in the top of the fourteenth inning. When Wally Backman singled, scoring Strawberry, I implored the great Yankee catcher who has been credited with the idiom of discussion: "Let it be over now, Yogi."

No way! The baseball gods determine the termination of play.

Houston's Hatcher sent one deep down the leftfield line off Met reliever Jesse Orosco—score tied.

"It ain't over until it's over."

In the sixteenth Strawberry doubled—"Now that's like my guy Duke," I said. The skies were brightening now; Ray Knight singled him home.

We took the lead again, and guess what, we're not through. A wild pitch and a Len Dykstra single produced two more runs.

"We're safe now," uttered Susan.

"No, no, don't say that. We need three outs, don't jinx it."

Orosco started his third inning of relief with a three-run cushion and a strikeout of the first Houston batter is worth a "Thata baby Jesse."

"Please, Yogi, let it be over." Now Susan was imploring the Hall of Fame catcher who won three MVP awards.

Walk, single, and yet another single, and the Met lead was cut to two. Davey Johnson stuck with Orosco and was rewarded as the left-hander records the second out on a ground ball to Hernandez. The winner of several Gold Glove awards fielded the baseball cleanly and threw to second base for the force-out.

"Way to go, Keith, keep that tying run from scoring position."

Yogi caused more pain, a single scored the Houston sixth run.

"It ain't over until it's over."

Please, Mr. Berra, please. C'mon, you may have had your glory in Pinstripes, but remember, you played and managed for us also.

A sigh of relief from Susan and a "thank you Yogi" from Joey soon followed.

Orosco struck out Kevin Bass swinging.

It's finally over—Mets 7 – Astros 6. The Mets were going to the World Series.

Joey Kowalski got the phone call he expected.

"I tolerated that column, Kowalski, only because you had all the references to the best catcher of all time."

"I kinda thought you'd like it, Lou."

"By the way, Kowalski. It's a good thing that your guys won. If not, they would have had to face Mike Scott again in game 7. That bastard only gave up eight hits and one run in his two complete game victories."

"You got that right, Marciano. He was the MVP of the Series."

3

It would be New York versus Boston in meaningful baseball games again. No, it would not pit DiMaggio or Mantle versus Williams, nor would you be seeing Guidry facing Rice and Yaz. There would be no encounter between Pudge Fisk and Thurman.

The Red Sox would not be facing their hated rival from the Bronx; rather they would be playing their road games in Queens. The 1986 World Series would have the Paul Revere crew against the New York team from the easterly most New York City borough, the Mets.

The Beantown boys had miraculously survived their American League championship series against the Angels. The game 5 victory on October 12, certainly was another "It ain't over until it's over" encounter.

Trailing in the top of the ninth inning by a score of 5–2, it was becoming apparent that the curse of the Bambino would once again haunt the loyal Sox rooters. Not only were they behind in the game, they trailed the California squad from Anaheim three games to one in the series.

"Turn out the lights, the party's over." The Don Meredith refrain on Monday Night Football seemed apropos.

"But it ain't over until it's over."

Two home runs, each with a man on, propelled the Red Sox to a 6–5 lead. The congratulations of the Boston rooters were heaped upon

Don Baylor and Dave Henderson. The latter's blast off of Donnie Moore, the Angels star closer with two outs.

So that was the ball game right? Wrong. "It ain't over until it's over."

The Angels tied the game in the bottom half of the inning.

In the second extra frame, it was Dave Henderson again, this time with a clutch sacrifice fly.

Yogi then gave the Red Sox nation a break. Calvin Schiraldi set down the Angels in order in the bottom of the eleventh to preserve the victory.

Boston had life, but still trailed the Series three games to two.

Was the Babe just teasing the Fenway Park faithful when he allowed the Sox to win the next two games there and secure the AL pennant?

4

The pre-Series analysis in the New York and Boston newspapers touted the stalwarts from each team and speculated on who the difference makers might be.

The first game lineups at Shea Stadium on Saturday, October 18, were revealing; several identifications were noteworthy.

Neither Doc Gooden nor Roger Clemens was scheduled to be their teams starting pitcher. Gooden had started game 5 versus the Astros on the fourteenth, and Davey Johnson preferred to give his stud right-hander another day's rest. Similarly, Clemens had started and won the deciding game 7 against the Angels and would be on full rest if he started game 2 against Gooden.

Bruce Hurst, the Red Sox veteran left-hander, would get the start against a very well-rested Ron Darling.

Don Baylor, who led the Sox with thirty-one home runs during the regular season, sat out since there was no DH in the games played in the National League Park.

The lineups:

New York Mets:

Boston Red Sox:

New York Mets	Boston Red Sox
Mookie Wilson LF	Wade Boggs 3B
Lenny Dykstra CF	Marty Barrett 2B
Keith Hernandez 1B	Bill Buckner 1B
Gary Carter C	Jim Rice LF
Darryl Strawberry RF	Dwight Evans RF
Ray Knight 3B	Rich Gedman C
Tim Teufel 2B	Dave Henderson CF
Rafael Santana SS	Spike Owen SS
Ron Darling P	Bruce Hurst P

The Shea Stadium crowd of over fifty-five thousand witnessed an excellent performance by Darling. Over seven innings, the fifteen-game winner during the regular season, allowed just three hits and no earned runs. His pitching line also displayed eight strikeouts and three walks. Unfortunately, he did allow an unearned run, the result of a Tim Teufel error in the seventh.

This proved costly as Bruce Hurst allowed no runs over eight innings and was credited with the victory after Calvin Schiraldi hurled a scoreless ninth for the save.

The following morning several of the New York and Boston papers had a photograph of Keith Hernandez and Wade Boggs shaking hands by the batting cage prior to the game.

Keith Hernandez shook hands with Wade Boggs of the Red Sox prior to game 1 of the 1986 World Series.

Hernandez, widely acclaimed as the best fielding first baseman in baseball, was also a former NL MVP and batting champion. Boggs, a stellar third baseman, was revered for his hitting prowess. He won his third AL batting title in 1986, with an average of .357.

Game 2 was no better for the Met fans as a second throng of fifty-five thousand–plus exited the Flushing, Queens, ballpark with the bad taste of a 9–3 defeat.

The Gooden-Clemens matchup did not live up to the hype. The two young studs were even below pedestrian.

	I		H	R	ER	BB	SO
Dwight Gooden	5		8	6	5	2	6
Roger Clemens	4.1		5	3	3	4	3

Gooden gave up home runs to Dwight Evans and Dave Henderson and took the loss.

The Mets headed to Boston needing to win at least two games at Fenway Park to return to Shea Stadium with a chance to capture their second World Series title.

Late that evening Lou Marciano called Bob Murphy. The two would usually have been together, along with Joey Kowalski, watching the Giant game on a football Sunday. On this particular autumn day both Bob and Lou had family commitments, and Joey used his sportswriters pass to be at Shea Stadium.

"Do you believe that Phil had four interceptions today?"

"No way should we have lost to Seattle, Lou. We outgained them in rushing and passing. You are right though, the INTs killed us."

"Are you ready, Murphy?"

"For what?"

"A Marciano prognostication."

"Why don't you just say prediction, you asshole. Let's hear it."

"That's the last freakin' game we are going to lose all year."

"From your lips to God's ears, Lou."

"So, Bob, do you think Joey is shitting his pants with the Mets down two games to none and now having to go to Fenway?"

"After his boy Dwight laid an egg, it will be interesting to see if he writes a column about the Mets tomorrow. The Red Sox had eighteen hits. By the way, who is the Yankee fan rooting for in this Series?"

"I am kinda hoping that they would both lose. I can't stand either team."

Bob responded. "I am not much of a professional baseball fan anymore. It's not the same without Willie around. For Joey's sake I'm pulling for the Mets."

Roger Clemens, 23 (left), and Dwight Gooden, 21, were despite their ages two of the best pitchers in baseball as they were photographed after being selected to represent their respective leagues in the 1986 all-star game. The two right-handed phenoms also faced off in game 2 of the 1986 World Series. Surprisingly, neither pitcher lasted past the fifth inning.

5

The Mets accomplished what they needed to do to survive—that is, be victorious in two of the three encounters in Boston. The outcome could have been better, however, as New York tied the Series at two games apiece before submitting to the Sox in game 5.

Game 3—Bobby Ojeda pitched seven strong innings, allowing five hits and a solitary run. Roger McDowell tossed two perfect innings to close the deal.

Len Dykstra led the Mets assault against Red Sox right- hander Oil Can Boyd. The spunky center fielder had four hits for the day, including a leadoff home run in the visiting team's four run first inning. **Mets 7 – Red Sox 1**

Game 4—Met catcher Gary Carter garnered three of the Mets' twelve hits; two of which afforded him with the opportunity to tour the bases in a casual trot. Ron Darling was unscored upon over seven innings despite allowing ten base runners; six of which were free passes.

The Mets had a minor scare in the eighth inning as Boston tallied twice against Roger McDowell before Jesse Orosco recorded the third out of the inning. The Met lefty reliever also hurled a scoreless ninth.

Wade Boggs and Bill Buckner were each hitless in five at bats. The Mets had a second relatively easy time of it at Fenway. **Mets 6 – Red Sox 2.**

The Boston papers, initially on a high after the two victories at Shea Stadium, now had to concern themselves with facing Dwight Gooden and the prospect of returning to New York down three games to two.

Game 5—The Red Sox needed a stellar performance from a starting pitcher. Bruce Hurst had been masterful in the opening game and took the mound with four days rest. The tall left-hander shut down the Mets without a run over the first seven innings before allowing solitary runs in the eighth and ninth. His complete game victory was just what the doctor ordered for Boston.

Dwight Gooden was not a mystery for the Beantown hitters. The right-handed phenom was led to the showers by Davey Johnson after facing three batters in the fifth inning without recording an out. His final line was a very uncharacteristic four innings, nine hits, four runs, three earned, with two walks and three strike outs. **Red Sox 4 – Mets 2.**

Now the Boston papers clamored for the end of the curse. "Enough already, Babe, it's our time."

The Red Sox would have their own youthful right-handed all-star, Roger Clemens, available to bring home the bacon. He would be well rested for the Saturday start, having last pitched in game 2 the Sunday before.

6

The agony on Joey Kowalski's face was evident as he arrived at the home of Bob Murphy to watch game 6 of the baseball championship. Lou Marciano joined his two good friends,

"Have a beer and relax, Kowalski, do you want a Bud or a Heineken?" inquired the host.

"Better give him a shot with the beer, Bob, he's trying to figure out what his team has to do to beat Clemens."

"No problem, Lou, I have a bottle of Jameson's opened, I'll pour us each a shot."

"You guys had better be rooting with me tonight. I could have gone to Shea but chose to be with my two best friends for luck."

"Just for you, Kowalski, I hate both teams, as you know. There's a first time for everything, I guess. Let's go, Mets!"

"I'll join you, Lou," added Murphy, "Meet the Mets, greet the Mets. By the way, there are pizzas in the kitchen, if you're hungry."

In the top of the first inning, after a two-out double by Dwight Evans scored Wade Boggs, Joey implored Bobby Ojeda to "settle down and get this third out."

Following another clutch two-out hit, a Marty Barrett single in the second inning for the Sox second run, Kowalski was back on his feet.

"C'mon Bobby, get Buckner, we can't afford to fall any further behind with Clemens on the mound."

The way the Boston right-hander out of the University of Texas was throwing, his words were prophetic. Clemens had four strikeouts after the first two innings, allowing only one base runner, a walk to Daryl Strawberry.

"Clemens looks tough, Joey. You'll need to get his pitch count up and hope you can get to the Boston bullpen."

"Marciano has a point, Joey. Roger is money tonight."

The score remained 2–0 for the visitors as the home team bats in the bottom of the fifth inning.

"It's the bottom of the fifth, a common occurrence at the Marciano family cousin reunions," uttered a smiling Lou.

Joey would typically have appreciated Lou's wit—not tonight. He remained devoid of his customary grin.

"C'mon, Daryl, start us off."

Strawberry listened, drawing a leadoff walk, and, with Ray Knight at the plate, stole second base. A Knight single to center field brings Joey to his feet as Strawberry scored the Mets' first run.

"OK, nobody out, let's keep it going, Mookie."

Wilson singled to right field and Ray Knight advanced to third base as the usually flawless fielding Dwight Evans did not handle the ball cleanly and was charged with an error.

"You have to pinch-hit for Santana in this spot," interjected Lou.

The coach of the St. John's varsity squad concurred. "It's a no-brainer. This may be the only shot the Mets get against Clemens."

Kowalski was in full agreement. "Johnson will probably send up Danny Heap in this spot."

The Met fan was right on point as the New York shortstop, Rafael Santana, took a seat on the bench.

The ensuing Red Sox double play afforded the opportunity for Ray Knight to score the tying run but effectively killed the inning. Davey Johnson decided not to use a second pinch-hitter for Bobby Ojeda, who grounded out.

"I agree with Johnson. Two out and a runner on first in the fifth inning, too early to use another guy when you have already tied the score."

Joey and Lou agreed with Bob's assessment.

Ojeda retired the Red Sox in the sixth, allowing just a single, and Clemens looked powerful, recording his seventh and eighth strikeouts in the bottom half.

"This would be a lot more fun if we could break your balls, Kowalski."

"You're right, Marciano, you owe us big time, Joey."

The Met manager decided to call on his right-handed reliever, Roger McDowell, to start the seventh inning. Bobby Ojeda had done a credible job, holding the Sox without a run from the third through the sixth after allowing the solo runs in the first two frames. Three of the first four batters would be hitting from the right side of the plate, so removing the left-handed Ojeda for the right- hander made sense.

The dreaded leadoff bases on balls to Marty Barrett had Joey Kowalski in a frenzy. "No way, Roger, you just can't walk that guy."

Buckner's ground out to second baseman Wally Backman allowed Barrett to advance one base. Then a critical throwing error by the

Met second sacker on a ground ball hit by the power-hitting Jim Rice positioned Red Sox runners on first and third with just one out.

The Mets are fortunate to get out of the inning, allowing just one unearned run. Jim Rice was thrown out at home plate by Mookie Wilson after a single through the SS-3B hole by Rich Gedman for the last out of the inning.

"That was big for you guys, Kowalski, really big."

"Not really what I would call a 'strength versus strength' scenario. Mookie's arm versus Rice's legs. The third base coach had to send him though."

Bob and Lou offered their commentary as Joey wondered if his team could generate another run off of the Red Sox ace. Not so in the bottom half as Clemens retired the Mets in order.

The top of the eighth inning was a cause for disagreement by the TV commentators and the three astute baseball aficionados watching the game.

Dave Henderson, the Red Sox number 7 hitter, led off the inning with a single off McDowell, and Spike Owen, the weak-hitting Sox shortstop, was the scheduled hitter.

"Wow, McNamara has a tough decision. Does he leave Spike in to bunt, let him hit away or pinch-hit for him?"

The St. John's coach had laid the groundwork for a response from his two friends. Lou accepted the baton first.

"All I know is that there is no way that I am pinch-hitting for Clemens when I have a one run lead. I would have Owens bunt, but let Clemens hit regardless."

Joey wasn't so sure. "Another run for them would be big."

Spike Owens produced a successful sacrifice bunt. Henderson moved to second base with one out, and holding a bat in the on deck circle was Clemens. Would the Red Sox manager John McNamara let his power-pitching right-hander hit for himself, or opt for a pinch-hitter?

Boston was leading by a run. How important was it to seek an expansion of the lead at the expense of losing your ace pitcher? The St. John's head coach, Bob Murphy, was decisive with his thinking.

"I agree with Lou, no way I hit for Clemens. The guy is a horse and I ride him at least into the ninth inning. He just had an easy 1–2–3 inning in the seventh. If the score were tied, it would be different."

Kowalski added, "He's got Greenwell available, I think he is going to hit for him."

"Screw you, Kowalski, you just want to get Clemens out of the game. Tell the truth, would you really pinch-hit?"

"Nah, in actuality I'd let him hit, Lou. You figured me out."

McNamara chose otherwise. Mike Greenwell picked up a bat as a disheartened Clemens returned to the adulation of his teammates on the bench after a performance of seven innings, four hits, two runs (one earned), two walks, and eight strikeouts.

"Asshole."

"Dopey bastid."

"Good move, McNamara."

Bob, Lou, and Joey reacted to the decision. Only Joey was smiling.

As Roger McDowell sent Greenwell meekly returning to the Sox dugout following a swinging strikeout, Bob was on the case of the Red Sox skipper.

"Clemens could have done that, McNamara, you dickhead."

Two walks later, the first an intentional pass to Boggs, and Jesse Orosco entered for the Mets to record the final out of the top of the eighth inning.

Calvin Schiraldi was the new Boston hurler for the bottom half.

"OK, Joey, now you have a shot, here comes your token Italian."

Lou referred to seeing Lee Mazzilli striding to the plate.

"You may have preferred DiMag or Yogi, Kowalski. Shit, Rizzuto would work also, but I like Mazzilli in this spot for you guys."

Lou Marciano's words were prophetic as Mazzilli's ground ball found the hole into right field for a leadoff single. The Shea Stadium crowd was ebullient.

After a fielder's choice on a Len Dykstra bunt attempt resulted in runners on first and second with nobody out, the preferred option of Davey Johnson was apparent. Wally Backman sacrificed the runners to second and third.

Now another key decision for McNamara—does he allow his right-hander to pitch to the left-handed hitting Keith Hernandez, or walk the former MVP and let him face the right-handed all-star catcher, Gary Carter? Pick your poison, McNamara.

In actuality, perhaps the choice was evident. Hernandez was a .310 hitter for the season, while Carter, although the more prolific power hitter, was over fifty points lower at .255.

McNamara ordered Schiraldi to intentionally walk Hernandez, and Carter came through with a deep fly ball to left field, which scored Mazzilli and advanced Dykstra to third. Strawberry flew out to center field but the Mets had new life.

Entering the ninth inning the score was tied at three.

After Rick Aguilera induced Rich Gedman to hit into an inning double play, the New York Mets have a chance to win game 6 in the bottom of the ninth inning.

Alas, after a walk to Ray Knight and an error on a sacrifice bunt attempt by Mookie Wilson placed runners on first and second with nobody out, Schirladi retired Howard Johnson, Lee Mazzilli, and Len Dykstra in order.

Extra innings!

7

The top of the tenth inning was a harbinger for disaster.

A leadoff home run by the Red Sox hero in their pennant winning series against the California Angels, Dave Henderson, was only the start.

Aguilera was able to set down the weak-hitting Spike Owen and pitcher Schiraldi, but a Boggs double and a single by Marty Barrett had the Sox on the verge of their first World Series since 1918 as they led by two runs entering the last half of the tenth inning.

Was the end of the curse of the Bambino beckoning the Red Sox faithful?

The sullen faces of fifty-five thousand Met fans were evident after Schiraldi retired Backman and Hernandez, the latter on a deep drive to center field.

Hold on, haven't you ever listened to Yogi?

"It ain't over until it's over."

Joey Kowalski stirred slightly after Gary Carter's single gave the Mets a ray of hope. The tying run was at the plate. Could Daryl Strawberry produce the magic of one of his titanic blasts?

Well, if he were still in the game, he would have had the chance.

"Damn it, Johnson double-switched in the top of the ninth. Mazzilli went to right field and Aguilera was moved into the five hole. Davey has to pinch-hit. It's got to be Kevin Mitchell here."

Joey was correct. Mitchell, with twelve home runs in 328 at bats during the regular season, brought his muscular frame to the batter's box.

A single to center field now had the Met fans clamoring for another miracle comeback.

"It ain't over until it's over."

Ray Knight, perhaps to some more famous for being the husband of the noted golfer Nancy Lopez, who had received her second Associated Press Female Athlete of the Year Award in 1985, brought the Mets to within one run—a single to right center field, scoring Carter as Mitchell moved to third base.

"It ain't over until it's over."

Lou goaded his good friend Joey. "It's getting late, Kowalski, Susan will want you getting home."

Bob picked up on the Marciano ball busting. "Do you mind if we watch something else, Joey?"

Cursing was never a part of the Joey Kowalski vernacular. That is until now.

"Suck my dick, both of you."

Bob Stanley entered the game for Boston. Red Sox nation, predominantly in New England area homes and taverns, held their breath. It wasn't the British this time. "The Mets are coming."

The elation at Shea Stadium could not have been at a higher octave when Stanley uncorked a wild pitch and Kevin Mitchell crossed home plate with the tying run.

"It ain't over until it's over."

An eleventh inning seemed apparent as Mookie Wilson hit a routine ground ball toward first baseman Bill Buckner. Buckner was playing several steps behind first base, however, and knew that Wilson's speed was such that he shouldn't dally. No matter, you have to field the ball first.

As the baseball rolled under Buckner's first baseman mitt, Ray Knight, who had advanced to second base on the Stanley wild pitch, just never stopped running until he crossed home plate.

Mets 6 – Red Sox 5—there would be a game 7.

As he left the home of Bob Murphy, Lou Marciano noted,

"The Bambino just loves to bust the balls of Red Sox fans."

8

The rain on Sunday caused the cancellation of game 7. The respective managers now had options not previously available to them relative to their choice of a starting pitcher.

John McNamara felt as if he had struck gold. Bruce Hurst, the winner of games 1 and 5, now had three full days of rest and was chosen to take the hill in lieu of Oil Can Boyd.

Ron Darling was the initial choice of Davey Johnson to start game 7. He would have been on three days' rest. The rain out granted him an extra day and Johnson decided on Darling rather than a switch to Dwight Gooden, who had last pitched on the Thursday before against Hurst. Joey Kowalski wondered, why not Dwight?

The press seats at Shea included the Sports Chat columnist / assistant sports editor of the *New York Daily News*, Joe Kowalski. He would have set up his best buds, Lou and Bob, with tickets but each had other plans.

"Hey, I'll root for the Mets only because of you, Joey, but I really don't give a shit. I'm watching the Giants-Redskins game."

"It's football season. I'll be over to watch it with you, Lou. Is your brother coming over?"

The baseball-football confrontation on a Monday night was cause for consternation among sport fans around the country. Game 7 of the World Series pitted against the telecast of the staunch NFC rivals—the 6 and 1 Redskins facing the 5 and 2 Giants.

On the west side of the Hudson River at the Meadowlands, a Joe Morris eleven-yard scamper put Big Blue up 10–0 and had Lou and Bob giving each other high fives. Back in Queens, the Mets were causing agida for Kowalski and the throng of Met loyalists at Shea Stadium. They had witnessed a brief Ron Darling meltdown in the second inning.

Back-to-back home runs by Evans and Gedman and an RBI single by Boggs later that inning, staked the Sox to a three-run lead. To compound the problem, Bruce Hurst was masterful again and took a one-hit shutout into the bottom of the sixth.

At halftime of the football game and the Giants holding a 13–3 advantage, Lou and Bob chatted about their Met fan friend.

"Joey must be shitting a brick."

"Forsooth, Marciano, you got that right."

After getting the first out in the sixth, Hurst falters.

- Lee Mazzilli, pinch-hitting, singles
- Mookie Wilson singles
- Tim Teufel walks to load the bases
- Keith Hernandez singles in Mazzilli and Wilson
- Gary Carter hits into a force out as Wally Backman, running for Teufel, scores

Red Sox 3 – Mets 3

"It ain't over until it's over."

When Nancy Lopez watched her husband, Ray Knight, put the Mets up for the first time in the bottom of the seventh inning with a leadoff home run, the Shea Stadium crowd was in an uproar. The Metsies tacked on two more runs in the inning and led by three.

Although the Red Sox came back to score a two spot in the top of the eighth, the home team retaliated with two runs of their own in the bottom half.

At 11:26 p.m., Bobby Ojeda leaped for joy. His strikeout of Marty Barrett had given the Mets their second World Series championship.

Meet the Mets, greet the Mets!

Lou and Bob were happy for Joey but had to sweat out the Giant game. They were ecstatic as Joe Morris scored his second touchdown in the fourth quarter of a 20–20 game, this time from thirteen yards out. Morris finished the game with one hundred eighty-one yards on thirty-one carries as Bill Parcells's squad prevailed 27–20.

Joey, also a big Giant fan, had hit the daily double.

CHAPTER XI

I'M GOING TO DISNEYWORLD

1

Thanksgiving 1986 for each of three couples was spent with their respective families. Ironically, the guys were all at their in-laws.

Lou Marciano was OK with the arrangements, in as much as, Grace's parents, Angelo and Marie Caruso, had also invited his mom and dad.

The next day, the guys and their wives, each with babysitters available, met at Luigi's restaurant for dinner. The initial topic of discussion focused on the movie that the couples had gone to see the previous weekend, *Stand by Me*.

Bob was insistent that one of the classic songs featured in the film was "Great Balls of Fire."

"C'mon, don't you remember Jerry Lee Lewis singing that?

Joey was not convinced. "Of course I remember Jerry Lee singing the song, but not in the movie."

The girls each chimed in.

"Bob's right, honey, 'Great Balls of Fire' is one of the hits from that movie."

Janet supported Susan. "Unbelievably, Bob is correct. He usually always screws up when it comes to movie trivia."

"I'm with Bob on this one, Joey." Grace then added a challenge to the group. "Name three other hits from the film and the artists who sang them."

Bob was gloating. "I can give you one right off the bat. How about 'Yakety Yak' by the Coasters?"

Susan countered for the girls with one of her oldie favorites, "Let the Good Times Roll." "That song, my good friends, was performed by Shirley and Lee."

Janet was just about to respond when Grace questioned Lou as to his tranquility. "What's up, hubby of mine? It's not like you to be so damn quiet."

"Don't say anything yet, Lou. I have a third song," bellowed Janet. "'Lollipop.' I just can't remember who the group that sang it was."

The sportswriter/author came to the rescue. "That would be the Chordettes, Janet."

"You guys have passed the test and that was with nobody even bringing up the title song or Buddy Holly singing 'Everyday.'"

Lou, who still had not uttered a word, was prodded again by Grace and finally spoke. "Call me the sentimental Italian, but that movie really got to me. Rob Reiner is a great director. As you guys well know, the narrator is one of the kids who is now grown up and is an author. He reads a newspaper article about one of his good friends who has died. Those kids were about twelve or thirteen years old in the story, and it reminds me of our good times together when we were that age. I guess the difference is that we never lost touch and remained best friends."

"Who was the narrator, Marciano?"

"It was Richard Dreyfuss, Murphy."

Eventually the inexorable friends are conversing by gender. The guys are talking football and the gals are discussing their kids.

Lou overheard Janet telling Grace and Susan that she must make a visit to the ladies' room. Unbelievably, probably due to the diminutive facility, Janet proceeded on her own. He waited a few minutes and then identified that he had to ask the owner a question. His intent was to talk to Janet before she returned to the table. He waited in close proximity to the ladies' room and confronted Janet as she exited.

"Do you think we can bring up our brief liaison now?"

Janet was momentarily flustered. "OK, Lou, but let me do it."

The return to the table had Joey talking to the others.

"I'll have a column on the Giants and Jets this week. With both teams at 10–2, I'm gonna pose the potential of an all New York Super Bowl."

"Joey, are you sure the timing is right? The Dolphins blew the Jets out last week. Marino had Walton crying like a baby who lost his nipple. You'd be better off waiting a week. If the Jets beat the Rams and the Giants beat the 49ers in Frisco, then you'll have a story?"

"You have a point, Bob, I will wait."

Bob offered an alternative. "Why don't you write an article on the Jets bypassing Marino in the 1983 draft?"

Lou, now trying to casually rejoin the conversation, recollected the blunders of many teams who neglected to pull the trigger on the quick release strong armed QB out of Pittsburgh University.

"Marino was only the sixth QB taken in that draft. Can you name the five guys selected before him?"

After fifteen minutes Bob and Joey have correctly identified the quintet.

- John Elway
- Todd Blackledge
- Jim Kelly

- Tony Eason
- Ken O'Brien

"Not bad, you dopey bastards. By the way, Joey, don't forget about the teams who screwed up by not taking Marino earlier in the first round, if you ever write that sequel. Especially the Jets—they could have had him with the twenty-fourth pick. Instead they took O'Brien."

Joey pondered the Marciano analysis. "That would be a good 'dopey bastid' story."

Janet, without the confidence typically injected in her speech, asked if she can have everyone's attention. "I have something to tell you guys, an incident that I am not proud of. It occurred while I was married to Richard."

Bob responded. "You mean, 'dickhead,' don't you?"

"Let me finish, Bob, this is very difficult for me."

Ten minutes later the verdict regarding the half-hour affair between Janet and Lou on the evening of Grace's wedding to Tony Roma, a marriage that lasted three months and ended in an annulment, was in.

Susan was instrumental in convincing Bob, now married to Janet, and Grace, now married to Lou, that the action did not impact them at the time and should not be cause for consternation at present.

"Janet had fallen out of love with Richard and was hurting. She knew she couldn't seek out Bob since he had gone to the wedding with Cynthia. Lou was by himself and she sought him out as a friend."

Grace, perhaps only half-jokingly, glanced at Bob and has a request. "Hey, Bob, want to go in the back for a quickie. This way Janet and Lou won't be one up on us."

Lou was disturbed by his wife's remark. "Well, if you had waited for me and not married that mafia-connected whop, and Janet had more patience with Bob and not hooked up with that asshole Richard, it never would have happened."

Janet concurred with Lou. "It was my fault, Grace, not Lou's. In fact he was the one that thought we should let you guys know. I was really looking for Bob that night but he was all over that big-breasted bimbo Cynthia all evening."

Now Bob was incensed. "Who told you to marry that jerk-off Richard? I would have eventually gotten around to giving you the ring back then."

Joey was intuitive and knew it was time to change the subject.

"Listen, Bob, you and Janet and Lou and Grace are together now and that is all that matters. Let's move on. What are we doing for New Year's Eve this year?"

"Joey is right," said Susan. "Let's discuss New Year's Eve."

Lou took a deep breath. "I thought about that, Mrs. and Mr. Kowalski. What about going to Roosevelt Raceway and then out to dinner?"

Janet was all in favor of the suggestion. "I'd love to go to the Milleridge Inn, I've heard that it is decorated festively for the holidays."

Susan and Grace concurred, with the latter adding a question for her husband. "When was the last time you won anything at the track, oh husband of mine, who slept with my best friend?"

Lou was initially noncommunicative but realized that he must keep his wits about him. The Janet-Lou affair had to be dismissed.

"I won betting on the Belmont Stakes didn't I, Enrico?"

Grace's maiden name was Caruso, and Lou often called her Enrico when he sensed that humor was the medicine to cure a potentially volatile situation.

"Well, track maven, I'll remember the Enrico comment when you are looking for a little loving tonight."

Susan had an inquiry. "Is that the trotters at Roosevelt?"

Her hubby, Joey, responded. "Yeah, babe, like a horse and buggy, but with a guy using a whip encouraging speed."

Susan advised all that she would make reservations at the Milleridge Inn for New Year's Eve.

"My cousin has been there several times. She loves it. Is 11:30 p.m. OK?"

Lou and Bob both felt that would be fine since the couples would leave Roosevelt Raceway by about 11:00 p.m. and the Jericho, Long Island–based restaurant was only about five miles away from the track.

As they left the restaurant, brief discussions between the sexual transgressors, Janet and Lou, and their impacted good friends seemed to relieve any tension that may have existed in their friendships.

Janet was direct with her girlfriend. "Listen, Grace, it was my fault entirely. Lou acted as a friend."

Bob thought the event was rather humorous. He did not feel that Lou had compromised their lifelong friendship in any way.

"Hey, good buddy, how was Janet that night? All I can remember was sucking on those melons of Cynthia's and then burying the salami after getting back to her apartment after the wedding."

"Murphy, you really are an asshole."

2

The New York Giants had heeded the prognostication of Lou Marciano. After their week 7 defeat to the Seattle Seahawks, Big Blue ran the table—nine consecutive victories. As previously accounted, the first of these triumphs was against the Washington Redskins on the evening of the Mets game 7 triumph over the Red Sox.

The second half of the 1986 regular season had the G-men in Super Bowl form.

- Week 9: Giants 17–Cowboys 14 (at the Meadowlands)
- Week 10: Giants 17–Eagles 14 (at Philadelphia)
- Week 11: Giants 22–Vikings 20 (at Minnesota)
- Week 12: Giants 19–Broncos 16 (at the Meadowlands)
- Week 13: Giants 21–49ers 17 (at San Francisco)
- Week 14: Giants 24–Redskins 14 (at Washington)
- Week 15: Giants 27–Cardinals 7 (at the Meadowlands)
- Week 16: Giants 55–Packers 24 (at the Meadowlands)

The 14-2 record earned the Giants a first-round bye in the playoffs.

Joey Kowalski never did write his column about a potential Giant-Jet Super Bowl. The Jets failed to cooperate relative to maintaining a euphoric spirit regarding a contest between the NFC and AFC teams from the same city. Joe Walton's crew, after starting the season with one mere defeat in the first eleven games, had a minor collapse, losing the remaining five contests. They barely hobbled into the playoffs. Even their 35–15 wild card victory over the Kansas City Chiefs on the Sunday after Christmas failed to alter his thinking.

New Year's Eve was both pleasant and eventful.

The girls were delirious, each picking three winners in eight races at Roosevelt Raceway and pocketing over one hundred dollars.

Joey broke even with a last race exacta, bringing him out of the hole. His childhood cohorts were both winnerless.

"Where is Carmine Abbatiello when I need him?" "What the hell are you babbling about Marciano?"

"Well, Bob, if Carmine were still around, I woulda just bet him in every race and probably made some bucks. I can remember going up to Yonkers Raceway on several occasions with my father and brother. Abbatiello was the only driver my dad would bet on."

"Why did you say driver, Lou? Aren't they jockeys?"

"No, Janet, they are called drivers. Shit, and the girls all won, what a joke."

Bob opted for departure from the Westbury, Long Island, facility. "I need a freakin' drink, let's go to the restaurant. What time did you make the reservation for, Susan?"

All of a sudden, the previously joyous smile on Susan Kowalski's face turned into a frown never before witnessed by her husband, Joey.

"What's the matter, babe?"

Janet sensed a problem. "Susan, are you OK?"

Susan had tears in her eyes as she meekly uttered, "I forgot to make the reservations."

As Janet and Grace comforted Susan, Lou remained unconcerned.

"Let's just drive over there and see what happens."

"It's New Year's Eve, Marciano. That place gets jammed on the holidays, so you may as well forget about tonight."

"Don't sweat the small stuff, Murphy. Just make like Mario Andretti and get us over there."

3

The three couples arrived at the charmingly adorned restaurant at eleven fifteen. The Christmas decorations and lighting, which should have been reason for the pretty and warm smile of Susan Kowalski, to radiate the entranceway of the Milleridge Inn, were nothing but a tearful expression of failure.

"I'm so sorry, everyone."

Lou requested that the others go to the bar for a drink. "Get me an Absolut martini on the rocks with olives, Grace, I'll check out the reservation."

Grace shook her head in disbelief. "We don't have a reservation, genius, and the line is a mile long for a table."

"Who says we don't have a reservation? Maybe I called and you just didn't know it," responded Lou.

Lou Marciano looked at the line of patrons, all of whom were obviously seeking to be seated before midnight. He guesstimated that there were close to a hundred people.

He walked over to the reservation waiting table. There appeared to be a list of names that was being checked by a lovely lass, who then identified that a table was ready.

"Simpson party, table for four."

"Excuse me, miss, but I have been waiting at the bar for over an hour. Would you be so kind to check if the table of six for Marciano is ready? We are anxious to be seated. Thank you."

The search for the Marciano name was nowhere to be found, obviously with good cause; the table for six had, in actuality, never been requested.

"I'm sorry, sir, are you sure the table was reserved under the name Marciano? I can't seem to find it."

"I'm sure it's there," Lou said confidently, "please check again."

A second search yielded similar results.

"I'm very sorry, Mr. Marciano, your name is not here."

"Would you have a manager come over, please. This is ridiculous."

Upon the manager's arrival, Lou maintained his position with only a mild outburst. "What kind of a place are you running here?"

Five minutes later, Lou walked toward the bar and summoned Joey.

"Get everyone ready and then follow me back into the restaurant area. Tell them not to say anything until they get to the table. I mean nada, nothing, you capisce?"

Joey had seen many of Lou's acts before. He complied with his wishes.

As the six were finally seated at one of the better tables, close to the fireplace, Grace questioned her husband. "How the hell did we get seated before all of those other people?"

Bob saw a chance to use one of Lou's old standby lines. "He made them an offer they couldn't refuse."

Joey inquired, "All right, Marciano, how did you do it? It couldn't have been with a handout under the table, you lost everything at the track."

Lou smiled broadly. "Let's just say I told a little white lie. My mother always told me they were allowed as long as no one got hurt."

Susan got up and gave Lou a kiss and a big hug. She was still not sure what he did to enable the three couples to be seated comfortably twenty minutes before the New Year. However, she was cognizant of the fact that he had saved her tushi.

"I love this guy, Grace. Wanna trade?"

Grace smiled but doesn't respond. She thought to herself, *Lou has already had Janet and I, why not Susan?*

Lou then explained how he had misled the Milleridge staff into thinking that his name was placed on the "table waiting list" at about ten thirty and that his group was patiently waiting to be seated.

"It was easy. I just relied on what I learned playing pranks in grammar school and high school."

"Here's to my friend, Marciano. I won't even call you an asshole tonight."

"Thanks, Murphy, you asshole!"

The conversation then shifted to sports movies, with Lou Marciano raving about the movie that he and Grace had seen the previous week.

"You guys should have been with us when we went to see *Hoosiers*. It was a great basketball movie. In fact it may have been the best sports movie I have ever seen. Gene Hackman was excellent as the coach and Dennis Hopper stole the show portraying the drunken father of one of his Indiana High School players. Hackman brings him on as an assistant coach because of his acute knowledge of the opposing high school teams."

Joey and Bob were both favorably inclined to see the hoops extravaganza. Joey offered a baseball movie for discussion. "I loved *The Natural*.

Grace interrupted. "Barbara Hershey was in *Hoosiers* and I think she was in *The Natural* too."

Joey verified the statement, but unfortunately for the guys, the gals took over the conversation discussing their favorite actresses.

Bob was disgruntled. "What about *Slap Shot*?"

4

Joey Kowalski had come through again—two extra tickets for Bob and Lou to attend the Giant playoff game against the 49ers at the Meadowlands. Joey sat with his cohorts from the Press.

As Bob Murphy and Lou Marciano awaited the 12:30 p.m. kickoff, they were finishing their third beers, having consumed two each in the parking lot upon their arrival. The hero sandwiches of salami and provolone provided by Grace were not really a typical tailgate meal but satisfactory since it was just the two of them.

The Meadowlands scoreboard reflected the previous day's results. In the AFC, the New York Jets were defeated by the Cleveland Browns, 23–20 in OT. Surprisingly in the National Football Conference (NFC), the Giants NFC east rival, the Redskins, had put a hurtin' on the prior year's Super Bowl winner, the Bears, 27–13. The final score was even more astonishing since the game was played in Chicago.

It would be Joe Montana versus Phil Simms on the west side of the Hudson River; Big Blue established as three- point favorites.

"Montana can be tough, Lou, especially throwing to Rice and Dwight Clark."

"You got that right, Murphy, and he's got Russ Francis at tight end, and Roger Craig out of the backfield."

"What was the final amount we decided to bet?"

"We've got five hundred dollars each on Big Blue, Murphy. We laid three points."

"Our defense is playing great and Simms will throw a pair of TD passes. Add a TD for Morris and a field goal for Allegre. I like the Giants 24–13."

"Good score, Bob, I'll go along with you."

As Mark Bavaro snared a Simms pass over the middle for a twenty-four-yard touchdown, the whooping began. Bob and Lou high-fived each other and also the surrounding Giant fans from their second-deck seats on the thirty- yard line.

A first quarter San Francisco field goal was quickly forgotten after the early second stanza forty-five-yard scamper by Joe Morris put the Giants on top 14–3.

"Way to be Joe."

"Don't let up, guys, keep it going."

The order was reversed—Lou praising the diminutive in stature but physically solid Joe Morris and Bob requesting the home team to keep the pressure on their West Coast rival.

Not to worry. Simms' second TD pass, this time a fifteen- yard strike to Bobby Johnson, was followed by the Meadowland crowd going berserk over the play by number 56. Lawrence Taylor, acclaimed by many as not only the best linebacker in football, but perhaps the ultimate player on the defensive side in the entire NFL, pilfered a Montana pass and didn't halt his stride until he reached the end zone. The thirty-four-yard jaunt has New York on top 28–3, which remained the score at the halfway mark of the contest.

In the second half, Simms continued to spread the wealth. Touchdown throws to Phil McConkey, the former Navy star, and Zeke Mowatt, the second tight end, delighted the crowd further, and the second

Joe Morris TD, still before the end of the third quarter, was an identification that the Giants were reaching their peak as a football team at just the right time.

It became a "Jeff" fourth quarter. Back up QB's Jeff Rutledge of the Giants and Jeff Kemp of San Francisco replaced Simms and Montana in the 49–3 annihilation.

"We'll have to beat those fuckin' Redskins for a third time this year to get to the Super Bowl."

The identification by an adjacent fan was met with immediate responses from Lou and Bob.

"Hail to the Redskins, my ass,"

"We'll be at least a seven-point favorite, but we'll cover that easily. Bet your house on Big Blue."

Bob had the closing comment on this occasion. "I would have loved to play the Bears just to get even for last year."

5

Rose Marciano spent two days at Flushing Hospital. Lou's mom, with a history of high blood pressure, was released on Sunday morning and was thankfully home and relaxing before noon.

"Alfredo, get down my pots, I have to make sauce for my sons."

Lou and his brother, John, had picked up their mother from the hospital. The championship game ticket, secured by Joey for Lou, would also be used by Bob. It was a privilege to have his friend, Gerry Cooney, join him.

Back in Jackson Heights it would be a Marciano family affair in viewing the Giants quest to play two weeks hence in Super Bowl XXI.

What would more typically have been an "Alfredo, John, and Lou" observation of a New York Yankee telecast would be a pigskin analysis on the eleventh of January 1987.

Prior to the 4:00 p.m. commencement of the third meeting of the season between the Redskins and Giants, it was pinochle time. Lou's uncle Vinny joined his dad, brother, and Lou in the bid version of the card game. John and Lou were always in amazement at the expertise of their father and uncle while playing the Italian heritage game.

"Let's go, Lou, the bid is 350. Are you passing?"

"I'm thinking."

"John, your brother is even slower than you. Paint dries faster."

Al Marciano laughed at the pronouncement of his brother- in-law, Vincent, the boys' uncle and older brother of their mom. In actuality, the reason for Lou procrastinating wasn't because he was in deep thought. His focus was not entirely on pinochle because he frequently peeked at the TV to view the progress of the championship game between the Cleveland Browns and Denver Broncos.

By three o'clock the cards were put away and the four witnessed the miraculous drive led by John Elway to steal a victory from Cleveland. The four enjoyed the cold antipasto platter that Rose Marciano and John and Lou's Aunt Helen had placed in front of them. The viewing participants, except for Lou, all imbibed on scotch, Dewars White Label on the rocks.

"I could never develop a taste for scotch. I'll stick with an Absolut martini to start and then switch to Budweiser."

Dinner was served much quicker than usual. John and Lou did not want to miss a play. Al Marciano and Uncle Vin were not as quick to leave the dinner table.

The game ended with Jay Schroeder of the Redskins completing twenty passes for one hundred fifty yards against the meager Phil Simms's total of just seven completions for ninety yards. That was the good news for the visitors from Washington, DC.

The bad news was that the Giants thoroughly subjugated the Skins' in the twenty-two-miles-per-hour gusting winds at the Meadowlands. The Giants had an interception, a fumble recovery and four sacks in a 17–0 dominating performance. All three of the Giant-scoring plays occurred in the first half. A Simms eleven-yard toss to Lionel Manuel and a Joe Morris one-yard burst, combined with the Raul Allegre opening field goal from forty-seven yards, accounted for all the New York points.

The deceiving stats were the result of Schroeder having to throw fifty times: his counterpart put the ball in the air on a mere fourteen occasions. Morris carried the ball twenty-nine times for eighty-seven yards and his fullback sidekick, Maurice Carthon, added twenty-eight yards on seven carries.

It would be the Giants and the Broncos in the Super Bowl. The team the G-men had defeated earlier in the season would be their opponent in Pasadena two weeks hence.

6

The Super Bowl festivities were set. Joey and Susan Kowalski would play host and hostess. The sportswriter had opted against the flight out west. Several other *New York Daily News* reporters would fulfill the obligation.

An excerpt from the last Joe Kowalski Sports Chat column prior to the first New York Giant attempt to secure the Vince Lombardi Trophy produced broad smiles on the faces of Bob Murphy and Lou Marciano.

And it was inevitable that number 11 and number 56 would be at the Rose Bowl stadium for Super Bowl XXI. The Giants are playing the type of dominating football that has the Las Vegas sports book in a quandary. What may have been touted as New York being about a three- point favorite in the game has now ballooned to nine. My buddies Bob and Lou are adamant. Lay the points, it's a lock!

Lou called Joey that evening.

"Great column, Kowalski. By the way, my mom is making a large tray of lasagna for me to bring over to your house for the Giant victory on Sunday."

"Don't jinx it, Lou."

"Joey, as you identified in Sports Chat, it's a lock."

7

Would the Giants, a one-time NFL powerhouse in the late fifties and early sixties, thereafter plummeting to the nadir, regain the accolades of the New York faithful on January 25, 1987, in Super Bowl XXI?

The families of Bob and Janet Murphy and Lou and Grace Marciano arrived at Joey and Susan's at 2:00 p.m. Game time was scheduled for 4:00 p.m.

As the six children were bundled up in the Kowalski backyard, the two girls joining the boys in an unsupervised touch football game, the adults were partaking in alcoholic refreshments and in conversation about their respective things that they would either like to do or see happen before they are pushing up daisies.

"Well," said Janet, "I'd definitely like to go to Warsaw. My grandparents, all four of them, were born there. Other than that, I have always had a fascination about skydiving."

"Screw skydiving, my list includes a Super Bowl for the Giants, a Stanley Cup for the Rangers, and an NCAA championship for my Redmen."

"The first of those will hopefully be off your list by about seven thirty tonight, Bob," countered Joey. "I think my list includes the top spot as a sports editor and several more books."

Susan, although from a close-knit Irish family, surprisingly had visiting the Vatican and all of Rome at the top of her list. "Also, I would love to drive a race car around the track at Daytona."

Grace aspired to function in elected office. "I think that being a district attorney would satisfy my employment dreams. Other than that, you can add four or five healthy grandchildren."

Lou finally surfaced. "I don't really believe in those lists. Maybe, when I was a kid, I would give anything to meet Mickey Mantle. Now I am satisfied with my memories. I just want to see my kids grow up, get married, have their own kids, and live every day to the fullest, knowing that I am blessed with a great family and special friends. I guess Bob's first two identifications aren't bad though."

"Good thing you added that, Marciano. I would have had to call you a wuss."

"Kiss my butt, Murphy. And by the way, Susan identifying Rome and the Vatican had me recollecting the Tony Masi story. I may have told you but it is worth repeating."

Susan was supportive. "Let's hear it, Lou, I know that you haven't told me."

"Well, as I recall, Tony was at the Vatican and wanted to go to confession while he was there. He was divorced at the time and seeking an annulment. His girlfriend was with him but was not Catholic, so he sought the sacrament of reconciliation on his own."

Bob interrupted his good friend. "The sacrament of reconciliation? Who are you trying to impress? We are not in Sister Marie Angela's eighth-grade class."

"Shut up, Murphy, I did it for effect. As I was saying before Bobby boy had to butt in, Tony got on line to confess. There were only five people in front of him to see the priest he chose to bear his soul to, and the person directly in front of him was a nun. After thirty minutes, only the good sister remained before he would get to cleanse himself from sin.

"To his surprise that confession took fifteen minutes and he entered the confessional apprehensively.

"Bless me, Father, for I have sinned. It has been five years since my last confession."

"Welcome back, my son. Are you here visiting?"

"Yes, Father, with my girlfriend. Rome is truly a beautiful city, and the Vatican is quite remarkable."

"Well, my son, before you begin purifying your soul, can you answer a question?"

"Certainly, Father."

"Are you having sexual relations with this woman?"

Tony paused; the inquiry having caught him off guard.

"Well, yes, Father, I am."

"*Get out!*"

"Excuse me, Father?"

"I said, *get out*. I will not allow you to continue while you are having relations outside of the sacrament of matrimony. *Get out!*"

Susan, Janet, and Grace were hysterical. Bob and Joey, who vaguely remembered the story, were laughing anyway.

Once the levity subsided, a tray of appetizers was devoured, and the guys readied themselves for the kickoff. The girls chatted in the kitchen and then got the kids settled with hot dogs and french fries.

The four young boys eventually joined their fathers to watch the game—that is, while their attention span lasted. A caution from Janet was presented to her husband and Lou. "Watch your language, you two."

The identification was tested early.

"Block the freakin kick, you guys."

The request was denied. The forty-eight-yard field goal attempt of Rich Karlis went through the uprights for a 3–0 Denver lead.

Soon thereafter Bob, Lou, and Joey were on their feet. Phil Simms connected with the Giant second tight end, Zeke Mowatt, for a six-yard score and a 7–3 New York lead.

"Let's blow them out now. C'mon, Lawrence, put Elway on his ass. Sorry, kids, I meant hieni."

Lou's son Marc laughed the loudest. "Sometimes my dad asks Scott and me. 'How's your hieni, is it nice and shiny?'"

Fortunately the youngsters were out of the room and playing with the two girls when John Elway ran into the end zone from four yards out on a quarterback draw from the shotgun formation to regain the lead for the Broncos at 10–7.

"That bastard should have signed with the Yankees, then we wouldn't have had to put up with this shit."

"It's about time we took control of the effin' game," countered Lou.

"Did you guys lay nine points?" Joey inquired.

"We bet straight up with that asshole Harry," answered Bob. Each of us gave him twelve to five, our one thousand two hundred dollars to his five hundred dollars."

"It should be like taking candy from a baby," added Marciano.

Fortunately, a Rich Karlis field goal attempt from just beyond extra point range, twenty-three yards, was no good, and the score had the white-shirted Broncos clinging onto a three-point lead.

"We dodged a bullet there," noted the *Daily News* assistant sports editor.

After a thirty-eight-yard punt from the Big Blue forty- seven-yard line placed the ball at the Bronco 15, Lou was on his feet.

"Now is the time. Let's play some Giant defense."

Bingo! The second sack of the series was in the end zone. Veteran defensive end, George Martin, accounted for the safety bringing down the star QB of the mile-high city squad to bring the Giants within one point. A second Karlis missed field goal, just before half time, from the "must make" distance of just thirty-four yards, was viewed in Lou's mind as a harbinger of what was to come about in the second half.

"What a shithead, and he was one of the most accurate kickers in the NFL this year. That can't bode well for those pecker-heads."

Meanwhile back in the kitchen the girls were preparing a few appetizers for the guys to pick on and holding one of their incomparable conversations.

Janet posed a question for her two sister-like friends. "Hey, girlfriends, do you think that we have a more special relationship than the guys?"

Susan looked at Grace and then responded. "Well, Mrs. Murphy, that could be the query of the year. What made you ask?"

"I don't know. Probably because Bob is always going on and on that he, Joey, and Lou would do anything for each other."

Grace interjected. "Is that all it takes? I wouldn't hesitate to be there for you two. I hope you both realize that. We've been best friends since the third grade."

"I thought it was second grade. No, I guess you're right, Grace. I knew you and Susan in second grade but thought you were both stuck up. We didn't become friends until the year we had Sister Josephine and she threw us all out of class for talking."

The three began howling in laughter, and Susan then summoned Janet and Grace to her. She placed her arms around each and her demeanor turned serious.

"I am so happy that you guys are my friends. I relish our relationship and know in my heart that we will be like sisters for the rest of our lives."

"You got that right, Mrs. Kowalksi" was the Grace rejoinder.

Lou, standing outside the kitchen, overheard the entire conversation. He decided not to say anything.

The second half kick off was run back by the Giants to their own thirty-seven-yard line. The ensuing drive was indicative of what Bob, Lou, and Joey expected from the game's inception. After a gutsy two-yard QB sneak on fourth down and one from the Giants own forty-six yard line by Giant backup QB, Jeff Rutledge, kept the drive alive, Phil Simms took over. Conducting the orchestra of a fluid Giant offense, he completed four passes, the final toss a thirteen-yard touchdown pass to Mark Bavaro. The Giants now led 16–10 and would never trail again.

A three play and out sequence for Denver and New York was back in business. Although slightly disheartened after the Broncos held Joe Morris to a one-yard pickup on a third and three from the Denver five-yard line, Raul Allegre added the short field goal for a nine-point lead.

A second consecutive Denver punt without netting a first down put Phil Simms back behind center. The nascent Giant superiority was becoming apparent. Five plays later, Morris scored from the one-yard line. The key play of the drive was a flea-flicker, Simms to Phil McConkey for forty-four yards. Giants 26 – Denver 10.

"Damn, Phil looks smooth out there."

"Remember when he was drafted as our first round pick in 1979. We wondered if he could become a franchise QB. I think there is no doubt about that now."

Bob and Lou concurred with Joey's assessment.

The snowball continued to roll downhill as Elvis Patterson picked off an Elway pass and the Giants put another six on the board in short order. A McConkey six-yard catch after a deflection off of Bavaro had the Kowalski household in an uproar.

Grace and Janet now began their own version of jubilation, happily gesticulating like cheerleaders with the knowledge that their husbands would each profit by five hundred dollars with the Giants victory.

"Looks like you and Bob split the bill with Lou and I the next time we go to Luigi's."

Susan liked the sound of that. "Luigi's, my favorite restaurant with my favorite people. What could be better?"

Ottis Anderson capped the Giants scoring on a two- yard run. The forty-seven-yard TD pass from Elway to Vance Johnson was never a real cause for concern. It was a convincing 39–20 victory for the G-men.

The team assembled by General Manager George Young, guided with a forceful hand by the coaching of Bill Parcells, and led on the field by number 56, Lawrence Taylor from the defensive side and number 11, Phil Simms, on the offense, had captured their first Lombardi Trophy.

Simms, with final stats of twenty-two completions in twenty-five attempts for 268 yards and three touchdowns was named the game MVP. Bob, Joey, and Lou sang the praises of the Giant who made his living throwing the pigskin.

"That was one of the best games I have ever seen a QB play."

"Simms was unbelievable."

"If he had a top outside receiver like Montana has in Jerry Rice, he'd be acclaimed at that level. Our best receiver is a tight end."

All the kids gathered round for what their fathers say was soon to come; the TV commercial featuring the MVP winner.

"Phil Simms, you won the MVP and where are you going?"

"I'm going to Disneyworld."

"Hey, Lawrence, I'm going to Disneyworld." A jubilant Phil Simms (left) hugged his all-pro linebacker teammate, Lawrence Taylor, after the Giants 39–20 victory over the Denver Broncos in Super Bowl XXI. Simms was the unanimous choice as the game MVP with one of the most dominating performances by a quarterback in Super Bowl history. He completed twenty-two of twenty- five passes for 268 yards and three touchdowns, without a single interception.

CHAPTER XII

FAMILY OF FRIENDS

1

The euphoria at the Kowalski home continued as the kids haunted Joey and Susan. It additionally carried over to the homes of both the Murphy's and Marciano's.

The kids of each had a common thread, asking the question,

"When can we go to Disneyworld?"

The six kids were now all Disneyworld ready.

- Grace Janet Kowalski, named after Grace and Janet, of course, would celebrate her eighth birthday on St. Patrick's Day.

The three boys were destined to share a friendship similar to their fathers.

- Christopher Joseph Kowalski would be six in April.
- Marc Anthony Marciano was to celebrate his sixth birthday in May.
- David Joseph Murphy would be six in June

And the two youngsters of the group:

- Scott Jonathon Marciano was already a better ballplayer than boys a year or two older even though his fifth birthday would not be until October.
- Gabrielle Murphy acted and appeared to be well beyond her years as her November birthday number cinco approached.

By the end of February, the plans for the three families were set. One week at the Contemporary Hotel at Disneyworld was scheduled for the last week in June.

Lou Marciano suggested that his nieces Jennifer and Kerry come along for babysitting responsibilities. All three couples agreed that Lou and Grace would get a suite with a second bedroom for the older girls.

The Kowalskis and Murphys were insistent on sharing the additional cost. In actuality, an equitable distribution for the larger room would never be cause for consternation among them. After all, they were even closer than most families—a family of friends.

2

Lou Marciano had several issues on his plate. He and Grace planned a move into Suffolk County, Long Island. A larger piece of property with a pool and a dog were their ingredients for the healthy upbringing of the two boys. Lou was also considering a position as the commissioner of public works in the county after the incumbent retired prematurely. For Lou, it would be a return to the public sector where he had spent the first fifteen years of his engineering profession.

Yet neither of these issues was foremost on his mind. His mother, Rose, had a minor reoccurrence of heart failure and at a very inopportune time. He was in the process of coordinating the move of his parents to a retirement village, and he was concerned about Grace, who was struggling with a decision to accept a position as the town attorney for the town of Brookhaven, a Suffolk County township and one of the largest in New York State.

All appeared to be going well as he played catch with his two sons on an early June evening after returning home from work. However, he was beckoned inside by Grace, and she handed him the phone. Tears were streaming down her eyes.

Rose and Al Marciano, his beloved parents, were gone. A collision on the Long Island Expressway with a tractor- trailer while driving home with their friends had killed all four. They were spending time looking at single-family homes at an eastern Long Island retirement village. Two couples, friends for over forty years, thought that such an arrangement, as long as they hey remained in close proximity to each other, would work. Now there would be no need.

Grace, as Lou knew for quite some time, was a pillar of strength as he and his brother, John, steadfastly made the required arrangements for their parents. Yet it became evident that beyond Father Mike and Sister Marie Angela, his spiritual advisors, there would have been no way of controlling his emotions over the three days that followed in Queens, New York, if not for his friends Bob and Joey. After all, they were his brothers also.

Two afternoons and evenings at Conway Funeral Home and a third day of mourning at the funeral mass held at St. Joan of Arc Church and ensuing burial at Calvary Cemetery were painstaking for the sentimental Italian.

Before Lou strode to the lectern to recite each of the poems he had written for the funeral mass, John hugged his brother. He had read each sonnet-like verse, advised his younger sibling of a few minor changes and additions, and was fully supportive of what his brother was about to undertake.

Those who knew Lou well were not surprised at his resolve as he eulogized Al and Rose Marciano at the church where he was baptized, confirmed, and married. Several ounces of Absolut vodka poured into one of his dad's hunting flasks helped quell his stream of tears.

Lou barely got through his heartfelt expression of love for his dad, who was well-known in the parish, having devoted thirty-five years as an usher at the ten o'clock mass, when he realized he had a second tribute to fulfill. He thought to himself, *This one is for you, Mom.*

> *Hey, Mom, a funeral poem is tough, it restricts my free prose.*
>
> *Yeah I know, keep it clean, OK, OK, Ma, give me a break, Rose!*
>
> *Let me commence by exclaiming what most of us present already know to well.*

Rose Marciano always had a kind word about others—yes, there is no need to dwell.

Her devotion as a wife, mother, nanny, sister, aunt, cousin, and friend

Was constantly strong, never wavered, and simply wouldn't bend.

She loved to cook, several dishes renowned, I wish all here could at least once try.

Her tomato sauce with meatball and sausage, eggplant parmigiana, and of course, potato pie.

So now let me ask my mom a few questions: like, have you been playin' Scrabble?

Can you watch Jeopardy *and the afternoon soap operas I used to call incessant babble?*

Do you have your chocolate-chip cookies, candy kisses, and ice cream?

Are you aware that I yearn to see your angelic face when I dream?

No more questions, Ma, just a statement that I know is shared by John's family, mine, and dad.

Having you as a mother, nanny, and wife has and will forever make us eternally glad.

After a slight pause, Lou, now with tears noticeable, had one final comment. "I wish that everyone could have such loving and giving parents as I have had the good fortune to experience. Good-bye for now, Mom and Dad. I love you, guys."

At the burial, Father Mike was invited to say a few words. He recalled consoling Lou's parents in 1958, when it was dubious whether or not Lou would awake from a coma.

"I have rarely seen such loving parents as Mrs. and Mr. Marciano."

As the family and friends exited Calvary Cemetery in Queens, Father Mike and Sister Marie Angela approached Lou and regretfully advised that they would not be able to attend the repast. Father Mike was cognizant of Luigi's restaurant and knew he would be missing out on some excellent Italian fare.

"You don't know how much I wish I could be there with you."

The good sister hugged Lou and handed him an envelope.

"Read this when you get a chance, Louis."

In the limousine, on the way to Luigi's restaurant, Lou opened the envelope from his eighth-grade nun at St. Joan of Arc grammar school.

> Dear Louis,
>
> I know that I am supposed to call you Lou, but your mother once told me that she would call you Louis often, for effect. This is one of those times.
>
> I just wanted to share a few thoughts with you about your parents, your brother, and your friends.
>
> First of all, I was just so impressed with your mom and dad. They both truly loved you and were always heaping praise on you. At the parent-teacher meeting in eighth grade, the evidence of a wonderful family life was imminently apparent. Your father was also of the opinion that I should give you a thrashing if you misbehaved. I know that you will miss them both terribly, but you

have fond memories to hold onto and should know that they will always be with you.

I don't really know your brother, John, very well. Yet I feel obligated to relate to you a story when you were in the coma. Your brother had walked out of your room at Astoria General Hospital and was getting a drink of water. He had tears in his eyes as he meandered away from the water fountain. I felt he was in pain and walked over to introduce myself. I told him one of the many stories of your mischievous class behavior and he smiled and seemingly relaxed. He told me that you had mentioned to him on several occasions that I was the best teacher he ever had. Then he said, "Pray for Lou, Sister. I don't want to lose my brother."

OK, Mr. Marciano, how can I not mention the other two jesters you have hung around with since grammar school? Robert and Jozef are truly special friends. Pardon me, I mean Bob and Joey.

I want you to do me a favor. Please relay to them that you three were always my favorites. I could count on the three of you to make every day at school an event to remember. Whenever I had to discipline any of you, it hurt me more than any of you. I am sure about that; but that is not why I bring them up.

When you were in the coma, I let the two of them leave class early on the Monday after your accident. They were not able to concentrate on their schoolwork; their thoughts were with you. Before they left Bob and Joey asked me to read the poem they had written. They wanted my thoughts on whether or not it was appropriate. In all my years of teaching, I had never read anything so touching. Those two confirmed to me what a special bond the three of you share.

My fondest memories from St. Joan of Arc are recollections of Robert Murphy, Jozef Kowalski, and you. Please impart my thoughts with them, and, Louis, thank you. Oh, one last thing. Stan Musial was better than Willie, Mickey, or the Duke.

God bless you.

Sister Marie Angela

3

Luigi Simonetti closed his restaurant to all patrons except those invited to attend the post-funeral dinner hosted by John and Lou Marciano.

The owner, in his broken English, was truly sincere, as he spoke with John and Lou.

"You motha and fatha were my very gooda friends, I will missa them."

"Dad would have wanted everyone enjoying themselves at your restaurant," noted the older brother. "He always had only the best things to say about you, your wife, and your daughters."

Moments later Bob Murphy came over and put his arm around John. "I love the food here, but nobody cooked as well as your mom."

Joey Kowalski joined Bob and John and related a story about Al Marciano.

"John, do you remember the Bucky Dent home run game when I watched it with you, your dad, and Lou? All he kept bringing up was how easy it would be to win the game if the Yankees had DiMaggio and Berra around."

As the three laughed heartily, Lou walked over to enroll as a fourth member of the conversation.

He was reluctant to bring up what was on his mind for fear of a tearful repeat of his eulogy experience. At a time when the atmosphere had turned upbeat, his reflections were focused on the fact that he had three, not one, brothers.

"Hey, you guys, guess what I'm drinking? This is my first ever Johnnie Walker Black on the rocks. It's in honor of my dad."

Soon thereafter, Janet and Susan ambled over to Lou, and each hugged him separately.

"You were truly blessed, Lou, your parents were great."

Susan seconded Janet's comments and added, "They would want you and your family to be happy, Lou. By the way, I was always amazed at how well Grace and your mom got along."

Grace heard her name mentioned and scurried over. "Talking about me behind my back, girlfriend?"

"Dat's right Caruso [Grace's maiden name], you gotta problem wit dat?"

Susan's attempt to mimic an Italian accent failed miserably but served the purpose of keeping the mood buoyant; those in earshot, particularly Grace, Bob, Janet, and Joey, laughed robustly.

Lou remained pensive; another issue had his focus. Then as if someone had flicked the switch in his cerebellum, Lou bellowed, "You guys, I've got it."

"You have what, Lou?" inquired Grace.

"The word."

"What word?"

"The word for friends who are like family."

"OK, Marciano, this should be good let's hear it" was the request of Bob Murphy.

"Yeah, Lou, what have you come up with now?" added Joey.

"*Framily.*"

4

That evening, Lou sat with his two boys on his lap in the family room. There was a sense of comfort emanating throughout his body as Marc questioned his father.

"Hey, Dad, Nanny and Poppy are in heaven, right? So if I'm good, I'll be able to see them again when I die."

"Yes, Marc, that's right, but you can talk to them every night when you go to sleep and say your prayers. They will be listening to you."

Scott looked to his father for a reaction similar to the one attained by his older brother.

"Me too, Daddy. Can I talk to them?"

"Of course, Scott."

Marc was perceptive with his next question. "Dad, will you be too sad to go to Disneyworld?"

Lou was amazed at the query of the six-year-old. "No, son, Nan and Pop would want us all to go and have a good time."

Scott smiled at the response and then inquired, "Hey, Dad, can you tell us the story about the time that you, Joey, and Bob beat those other three kids in the touch football game at the park. You know, the one where the other kids thought they would beat you pretty bad."

"Yeah, Dad, that's a good one," added Marc.

The storytelling was like an elixir for Lou. He soon had his sons jumping up and down and laughing as he conveyed the events of one of the many Jackson Heights sport episodes of Joey, Bob, and himself, which Marc and Scott found so entertaining.

When Grace beckoned the boys with "It's time for bed, you two," Lou backed up her appeal.

"C'mon, guys. Go put your pajamas on and I'll tell you another story."

"Yippee"—a simultaneous reaction.

Later that evening, as Lou and his wife were lying in bed, Grace sought an answer to the same question proposed earlier that evening by Marc. "Everyone wants to know if you would rather postpone the trip. They are concerned about you."

"Who's everyone?"

"Well, Mr. Sentimental, you know who, using the word you struggled to come up with for an eternity, your framily, Susan, Joey, Janet, and Bob."

"Grace, would you believe that Marc asked me that before? Nah, I'll be fine, my parents would want me to go and enjoy myself with you, the kids, and my framily. By the way, you never did tell me if you liked that word. Oh, the hell with it, that can wait. How about we play hide the pepperoni?"

"Now you're talking, honey. Thank God, the Italian Stallion is back."

"No more talking, Grace. Do you remember 'Johnny rides the pony'? Well, tonight, you're Johnny!"

FINI

Printed in the USA
CPSIA information can be obtained
at www.ICGtesting.com
JSHW020731121023
49836JS00002B/5